D0906587

# THE PERCEPTION OF DOTTED FORMS

# BOOKS BY WILLIAM R. UTTAL

# THE PERCEPTION OF DOTTED FORMS

## William R. Uttal
*Naval Ocean Systems Center*
*Hawaii Laboratory*
*Kailua, Hawaii*

**LEA** LAWRENCE ERLBAUM ASSOCIATES, PUBLISHERS
1987    Hillsdale, New Jersey                              London

_8700020146_

Lawrence Erlbaum Associates, Inc., Publishers
365 Broadway
Hillsdale, New Jersey 07642

BF
293
·U86
1987

**Library of Congress Cataloging-in-Publication Data**

Uttal, William R.
   The perception of dotted forms.

   Bibliography: p.
   Includes index.
   1. Form perception.   2. Dots (Art)--Psychological
aspects.   I. Title.   [DNLM: 1. Form Perception.
2. Visual Perception.   WW 105 U93p]
BF293.U86   1987          153.7'5              87-557
ISBN 0-89859-929-6

Printed in the United States of America
10  9  8  7  6  5  4  3  2  1

*As ever, for Mit-chan —*
*my perpetual perceptual inspiration.*

# Contents

# Preface

This book is the fourth in a series of research monographs reporting the results of a continuing study that deals with the perception of form in two- and three-dimensional space. I have been working on this study for over a decade since my interest in these problems was stimulated by a trivial laboratory accident—a broken wire that removed the horizontal sweep from a 5 by 7 dotted alphanumeric character display. The project has grown in complexity and theoretical richness beyond any expectations that I might have had the day the wire snapped. It has evolved into a major undertaking with a range of ramifications that I could not have anticipated at the outset and has consumed much of my professional life since. Every time that I expected the end of the study was near, a new stream of unanswered questions errupted that required attention. Nor am I yet sure that closure is at hand. As we shall see, there still are many unresolved issues concerning the perception of forms in general, and dotted forms in particular.

This project started out as an excursion into the detection of two-dimensional forms (Uttal, 1975) and then broadened to include three-dimensional forms (Uttal, 1983; 1985). The major change in the work that is reported here is that I have extended this work to include other visual tasks than detection—the one emphasized in the three earlier monographs. This volume explores the visual processes involved in discrimination and recognition as well as in detection. Nevertheless, the work is still highly constrained to a very narrow universe of discourse. My main concern is still with a single motivating question—*What are the specific attributes of visual forms that affect their visual perception?* The paradigm used is still the same—the visual processing of discretely sampled (dotted) stimulus forms when they are degraded by the addition of randomly positioned "masking" dots or visual "noise."

I have no aspirations to, nor do I make, any claims concerning the solution of the full range of problems of visual perception in spite of the fact that I have used these data as spring boards to the discussion of a wider range of perceptual issues than they alone define. Because my goals have been so specific and the context so constrained I believe that this work has been particularly fruitful and has accomplished some things that would not have been possible if I had used more complex scenes as stimuli or had delved into higher levels of visual information processing. The work I report here concerns itself with a very specific level of vision — an intermediate level between the processes of the receptors and the cognitive processes mediated by higher levels of brain activity. It is not just the stimulus material, but also the perceptual processes being assayed, that are tightly constrained in this study. On the other hand, a caveat: It may be that some of the visual processes being assessed are "cognitively penetrable," at least in part, but the main impression one derives from these experiments is of automatic, preattentive mechanisms at work.

The results reported here, therefore, are intense, but very narrowly focused. A great deal has been learned about how people see the kinds of stimulus forms (dotted three-dimensional surfaces) that have been studied here. However, something has also been learned that is a bit more subtle. Form vision is much more complex than most of my contemporaries seem to think. It is a humbling experience to be unable to discover universal rules that can be generalized from one visual task to another that may have seemed, a priori, to be very closely related. Furthermore, many of the popular computer-based models of visual perception may, in fact, be very poor models of what is going on inside organic visual systems. It is often unappreciated when some new and exciting algorithm is demonstrated how far the mechanical device has to go before it could claim to be truly homologous to the extreme complexity of human visual processes.

Because of this complexity, I have no sense of completion concerning this work. This monograph is but a progress report and there is much yet to be done. I hope my readers will be patient with me as I explore the psychophysical thicket in which I must admit I now still feel there is so much to be learned.

On a more personal basis, I should note that this past year I made a major move in my life. I left the Institute for Social Research and Department of Psychology at the University of Michigan for the Naval Ocean Systems Center's (NOSC) Hawaii Laboratory, fulfilling what was virtually a life long dream — to live and work in Hawaii.

I will always remember my friends and colleagues in Ann Arbor with the fondest regard. I am especially grateful to Tom Juster, Bob Kahn and the late Angus Campbell for allowing me to join and to participate in the rich intellectual and supportive social environment of ISR. It was truly an extraordinary experience and one that I will cherish for the rest of my life. Rensis

Likert, the founder of ISR, left a tradition behind that lasted for four decades as ISR became a lasting model of what the academy should be. That it was successful, stable, scholarly, productive, satisfying, and stimulating in the context of 40 years of "soft money" budgets, has much to say about the ways academic organizations are supported and operated today.

In my new post my work continues to enjoy the support and encouragement of a number of people. In particular, J. K. Katayama and J. D. Hightower provide an enthusiastic and exciting environment for all of the psychologists with whom I now have the pleasure of sharing these beautiful islands. My psychological colleagues in the Cognitive Sciences Branch — Ross Pepper, Hugh Spain, and Bob Cole (also of The University of Hawaii) and a few honorary men of psychology like Steve Wiker and Evan C. Evans III — have also made this move a happy and productive one.

The specific research reported here was supported by Work Request N0001458WR24281 from the Office of Naval Research. John J. O'Hare continues in his role as the ONR Scientific Officer for this project in its transition from the University of Michigan to NOSC-Hawaii. Indeed, my present work itself is continuous with that done in Ann Arbor. Some of the data reported here were actually collected while I spent the last of my twenty-two happy years there.

One of Ann Arbor's joys was Professor Wilfred Kincaid, now retired from the Department of Mathematics there as I now am from the University of Michigan's Department of Psychology. Wil was the intellectual force behind Experiment 7 which is reported here in a brief, edited form. It has been published in a more complete form as: The effect of 3-D orientation and stretching on the detection of dotted planes (Kincaid & Uttal, 1986, *Perception and Psychophysics, 39,* 392–396). I am grateful to Wil for his permission to publish a part of our joint effort here so that this volume and the series of monographs of which it is a part will be more than less self contained.

During the course of this research a number of people have assisted in the collection of data and its analysis or in programming the computers we use in our work. I am particularly grateful to Ramakrishna Kakarala, Larry Spino, Robert Radcliffe, Sharon Atkins, Cynthia Welke, and Nancy Davis who helped me bridge the transition from my post at the University of Michigan to the NOSC Hawaii Laboratory.

After a dozen books and the work of a good portion of a lifetime it is becoming almost redundant, but I would be less than complete in listing those to whom I am indebted if I did not point out that the main source of my inspiration continues to be my dear wife May to whom this book is once again lovingly dedicated.

W. R. Uttal
Kailua, Hawaii

# 1 Introduction

How do we see forms? That is the question that has guided and motivated my research for almost fifteen years. Nevertheless, it is a question that is so encompassing and so vague that it cannot be attacked empirically when stated baldly in this manner. To make any progress, this complex problem must be simplified so that its more specific corollaries become amenable to experimental manipulation. It is necessary to simplify the real world so that it becomes tractable to *controlled manipulation* and *computational simulation* — the best experimental and theoretical tools currently available to us in this interdisciplinary field of visual form perception. This is the fundamental method of science — the search for understanding the complex systems by examination of the nature of their constituent simple components. The necessity of this approach has been appreciated since Descartes (1637/1967) originally enunciated his rules of scientific method and John Stuart Mill (1838/1950) later proposed his "method of detail." The most important long range outcome of the emergence of this strategy of attempting to understand the complex natural world by analyzing it into its parts, it can be fairly argued, has been nothing less than replacement of speculation by experimentation and of opinion by testable proof.

In the spirit of the method of detail, we are led in this present work to study the specifics of form *detection, discrimination,* or *recognition* rather than the much more global and much less well defined concept called form *perception*. That, in brief, is the goal of this study: To determine the influence of the real or apparent properties of stereoscopically generated, three-dimensional forms on our ability to detect, discriminate, and recognize. We do so both by carrying out psychophysical experiments and by testing analytic models of the forthcoming results.

In an analogous way, the full richness of the pictorial scenes that usually impinge upon our visual receptors is simply too complicated for the scenes themselves to be used as the eliciting stimuli to explicate the microscopic details of how we see forms. Thus, in another great but much more modern tradition of psychological science, we simplify and abstract scenes down to flashes or lines or dots that only partially represent the full complexity of pictorial reality. This, in the spirit of Mill and Descartes, is done in order to carry out an understandable and controllable experiment.

These two great simplifications—the method of detail and, in one observer's words, "the graceful relaxation of stimuli"—are the bases of the work described in this monograph just as they were the guides for the studies described in its three predecessors (Uttal, 1975; 1983; 1985). The former is the reason for the use of the highly structured and simplified psychophysical procedures to be described. The latter is the reason that dotted abstractions of visual reality are used as stimuli. It is not too much of an exaggeration to say that the use of both strategies largely explains why considerable progress has been made in what otherwise is often a confounded and tangled research area.

Nevertheless, a price is paid for this increase in psychophysical and computational tractability. That price is that the conclusions that are drawn often cannot be generalized to what a priori may seem to be a closely related situation. At the outset of this monograph I wish to emphasize that any rules of visual perception that emerge from our empirical and theoretical studies are relevant and applicable only to the universe of dotted stimulus-forms and noise. In fact, there have been numerous instances in which the results obtained are qualitatively opposite when one compares experiments that use dotted and continuous forms respectively. For example, orientation does not affect the detection of dotted forms (Uttal, 1975) as it does continuous forms (Appelle, 1972). The enormous behavioral influence of what at first may seem to be but slight changes in the nature of the stimulus is characteristic of the pattern of results that have been obtained throughout this work.

There are other caveats as well that should be explicitly stated at the outset of this monograph. I cannot overemphasize my belief that the processes that are assayed by the kind of experiment reported here are characteristic of only a very narrowly defined level of vision. As many other students of the field have suggested, and as I tried to make clear in another book (Uttal, 1981), any visual perceptual experience is affected by many different levels of information processing starting with the absorption of light—the physical stimulus—by photo receptors in the retina and continuing through the cognitive manipulation of the conscious percept.

Some of the most important of the many levels of visual processing are summed up in the taxonomy presented in Table 1. This taxonomy suggests that there are several great differences in the various kinds, levels, or stages

TABLE 1
A process oriented taxonomy of visual processes. (From Uttal, 1981).

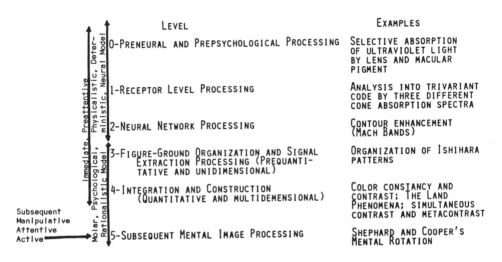

| | LEVEL | EXAMPLES |
|---|---|---|
| | 0-PRENEURAL AND PREPSYCHOLOGICAL PROCESSING | SELECTIVE ABSORPTION OF ULTRAVIOLET LIGHT BY LENS AND MACULAR PIGMENT |
| | 1-RECEPTOR LEVEL PROCESSING | ANALYSIS INTO TRIVARIANT CODE BY THREE DIFFERENT CONE ABSORPTION SPECTRA |
| | 2-NEURAL NETWORK PROCESSING | CONTOUR ENHANCEMENT (MACH BANDS) |
| | 3-FIGURE-GROUND ORGANIZATION AND SIGNAL EXTRACTION PROCESSING (PREQUANTI-TATIVE AND UNIDIMENSIONAL) | ORGANIZATION OF ISHIHARA PATTERNS |
| | 4-INTEGRATION AND CONSTRUCTION (QUANTITATIVE AND MULTIDEMENSIONAL) | COLOR CONSTANCY AND CONTRAST; THE LAND PHENOMENA; SIMULTANEOUS CONTRAST AND METACONTRAST |
| | 5-SUBSEQUENT MENTAL IMAGE PROCESSING | SHEPHARD AND COOPER'S MENTAL ROTATION |

of visual information processing. One of the most important is the great division between the attentive and the preattentive stages of visual perception. But, even within the preattentive category there are several discernible levels of visual processing.[1] Each of these stages of transformation essentially reflects the several different classes of theoretical explanation of the kind of mechanisms and processes that influence the final outcome—visual perception. Some visual effects can be attributed to the physics of the external world, some to the chemistry of the photoreceptors, some to the interaction of signals within the synaptic plexi of even the most peripheral portions of the retina, and some to much more complicated, preattentive processes for which the neural substrate is still obscure. It is arguable, but in my opinion it is certain that the combinatorics of such neural networks probably makes them inaccessible in principle.

The point is that I believe that the abstractions of physical reality—the dotted stimulus form—and the highly formalized experimental paradigm—a forced choice response to a nonrandom dotted form hidden in a random dot mask—that have been chosen as the experimental vehicles in the present study determine that most of the results obtained will reflect the properties of

---

[1]When I refer to these levels as "discernible," I am alluding to the fact that their effects are separable by an experimenter if the proper experimental paradigm or psychophysical assay procedure is used. It is likely, on the other hand, that the experiencing perceiver is not able to "discern" any difference in the processing stages; the perceiver is only aware of the outcome, not the processing means to that outcome.

an intermediate level of visual processing. This level is well above the processes best analyzed in terms of the chemistry and physics of the receptors but, in the main, not as high as the levels characterized as cognitive or attentive. This level is largely passive and automatic and occurs without effortful attention to the local details of the stimulus. The conclusions to be drawn some pages hence, therefore, speak mainly to this intermediate processing level. My warning is that it would be theoretically treacherous to overgeneralize them to other domains within which we already know that different rules apply.

I have inserted certain "weasel words" such as "largely" and "in the main" into the previous paragraphs because some of our recent experiments now suggest that some of the processes I originally thought were purely preattentive may, in fact, be to some degree "cognitively penetrable." I have more to say about this later, but for the moment I only note in passing that some intersubject and interexperiment differences in performance, particularly with regard to the recognition of stimulus form, suggest that something other than totally preattentive, automatic process may be at work here.

Another caveat should be expressed concerning the use of three-dimensional, stereoscopic material as stimulus forms in this study. While it has been extremely useful to use these forms to study a kind of form perception that is not often an object of research attention, *the genesis of the stereoscopic depth experience itself is not the problem of interest here.* The emergence of stereodepth from the invariances extracted from disparity cues by computational and neural mechanisms is a process that is beginning to be understood: (For example, see the work of Grimson, 1981; Julesz, 1971; Marr, 1982; Marr & Poggio, 1979; Mayhew & Frisby, 1981). Indeed, for this book the ability to generate depth from disparity is taken as a given. Rather *it is the perceptual manipulation of the perceived forms exhibiting that apparent depth generated subsequent to the solution of the correspondence and interpretation problems that is the research target of interest in this study.* By the correspondence problem I refer to the surprisingly difficult task, particularly in a random dot stereogram, of determining which dots in one eye's view are associated or correspond to which dots in the other eye's view. Without solving this problem, of course, the disparity between each pair of "corresponding" points could not be evaluated and an experience of apparent depth could not be generated.

By the interpretation problem, I refer to the task of determining the shape or form that is specified by the aggregate disparities of all pairs of dots in the stimulus scene. Neither of these tasks is explored here, nor are any of the conditions that might affect them manipulated in this study. We assume that the observers in our experiments solve these problems, but that they do so under controlled conditions that do not affect the solutions of the quite different tasks towards which our experiments are directed.

Though this fine distinction may seem to be a bit of verbal nit-picking, it does seem to turn out that the empirical tasks (i.e., experimental procedures) that are used in this study actually distinguish between these two sets of processes — correspondence and interpretation on the one hand, and detection, discrimination, and recognition on the other — in a subtle way. In the first case, disparity cues always produce a strong experience of depth in our experiments: The correspondence and interpretation tasks are, in other words, always solved because we provide good fixation signals. On the other, it is very often true that the strong induced experience of stereodepth does not produce a measurable influence on some task in which the observer is asked to manipulate or process another aspect of that apparent depth. This distinction is important because it is tantamount to the specification of an even finer taxonomy of the visual processes than has hitherto been proposed. Some very closely related processes that may be sometimes difficult to verbally disentangle turn out to be vastly different in their response properties.

The point I wish to emphasize here is that it is the properties of the *apparent* surfaces that are the problems of interest in this study, not the means by which the disparate images are brought into *correspondence* or how this disparity information is *interpreted* as objects in depth.

If the process of generating the stereoscopic depth experience is, at best, only of secondary interest in this context of the present study, a visual process of primary interest is the emergence of global form from discrete samples. How do we reconstruct the form when it is only partially presented by a constellation of dots? How is it that we see what are virtually complete "subjective surfaces" in three dimensions when the stimuli are composed of broadly spaced, discretely sampled, dots? The problem of reconstruction from samples has currently become one of the main foci of attention in my work, and I hope to report on that research soon. However, that potential work on reconstruction, which is more closely related to the interpretation problem, must be also distinguished from the other problems of more immediate interest in the present context — that of the detection, discrimination, and recognition of the reconstructed forms.

My final introductory caveat concerns what may ultimately be the major conclusion to be drawn from this work, one that can be formulated as a metarule that encompasses all of the other particular rules of dotted form perception that have emerged so far.

The Rule of Multiple Rules: Slight changes in procedure, stimulus material, or methodology often produce dramatic changes in the rules of dotted form perception.

That this metarule should emerge after so much experimental work is unfortunate, perplexing, counterintuitive, somewhat distressing, and certainly surprising. It has long been virtually axiomatic in psychophysical research that, if we are diligent in our collection of descriptions of the phenomena of vision, in the long run general principles of perception should emerge that will unify the outcomes of what often seems to be, at best, a random assortment of the results of small-scale and isolated experiments. It is not difficult to identify the intellectual forces to which we can attribute this optimistic and hopeful attitude: Psychologists, along with the rest of the scientific community, have long admired the progressive simplification the physical sciences have undergone as more and more general theories encompassing an ever widening range of physical phenomena have evolved. Without doubt, the recent progress in collapsing the various forces of physical interaction into ever more comprehensive and unified field theories stands as one of the greatest intellectual achievements of human existence.

As attractive as the proposition of ultimate generalization of other scientific enterprises may be, *the analogous hypothesis that psychophysical phenomena can also be so unified remains unproven and, indeed, largely untested:* Perceptual psychology remains a collection of small and seemingly unrelated empirical thrusts. Certainly, it is only in the rarest cases that psychophysical data obtained from different paradigms and different conditions have even been compared. Perceptual psychophysics has long been characterized by experiments specific to a microscopically oriented theory and by theories that either deal with a narrowly defined data set at one extreme or, to the contrary, a global breadth that is so great that data is virtually irrelevant to their construction.

The question posed here is — Is the lack of unification and the absence of truly comprehensive theoretical simplifcations (i.e., generalizations), which is so apparent in contemporary psychophysical science, a result of the youth of the science or does it reflect in some fundamental way the actual biological state of perceptual processes? Though the latter alternative is anathema to both experimental and theoretical psychologists and, from some point of view, a depressing prospect, it cannot be rejected out of hand. It is at least conceivable, that the perceptual brain-mind operates by means of subprocesses that are more independent and noninteracting than we had either anticipated or hoped. It is at least possible that superficially similar visual processes may be mediated by quite different underlying mechanisms. There have been so few instances in which a wide range of experimental conditions has been explored within the context of a single paradigm that there is actually little support for the antithesis — the idea that unification is, in fact, possible (regardless of how much such an outcome would have pleased us or satisfied William of Occam or Lloyd Morgan).

It must not be overlooked that there is also a possibility that the difficulty in identifying universal laws is due to differences in the perceptual strategies of individual observers. Evidence that such confounding exists can be found in the work of Ward (1985) in even such a relatively early level of processing as that of defining whether stimulus dimensions will be integral or separable in Shepard's (1964) and Garner's (1974) sense. Intra-observer experimental designs (i.e., using the same observer, to the extent possible, for all conditions of an experiment that are to be compared) are absolutely necessary, if it turns out that different rules are applied by different observers.

The evidence for independence of processes rather than generality in perceptual psychophysics is all too prevalent once one begins to look for it. As one goes from one laboratory to another, or from one research problem to another, there is rarely any linkage between the various outcomes. Furthermore, as we survey the history of psychophysical research, how very often we notice that the classic summary statements are clusters of almost independent rules (e.g.. Korte's, 1915, laws of apparent movement; Wertheimer's, 1922, enunciation of the Gestalt Rules of Grouping; Grassman's 1853, laws of color mixture; etc.) rather than a single unified conclusion tying together the separate results of experiments carried out in different settings.

Many psychologists have noted the absence of universal principles in perception. Hurvich, Jameson, and Krantz (1965) have suggested that this is the case in their insightful comment "The reader familiar with the visual literature knows that this is an area of many laws and little order."

V.K. Ramachandran of the University of California at San Diego has also raised the possibility that vision is characterized more as "a perceptual bag of tricks" than by great universal principles of perception (see, particularly, his editorial—Ramachandran, 1985). Of course, in any theoretical endeavor everything looks like a "bag of tricks" early in the game, before the unifying principles become evident. Nevertheless, an increasingly large number of observers of this field share the view that a widely diverse set of mathematical models may be necessary to describe what are viewed as a set of nearly independent visual processes. Grossberg (1983) makes the same point in listing the very large number of models presently used to describe visual processes and also alludes to a comment by Sperling (1981) in which the necessity of multiple formal models (and thus multiple internal mechanisms) is championed.

Another instance of idiosyncratic perceptual behavior is noted by Grossberg and Mingolla (1985) who, in pointing out that the way in which texture segregation occurs depends more on the "emergent perceptual units" than on the "local features" of the stimulus, warn that this "raises the possibility of scientific chaos." Grossberg and Mingolla go on:

> If every scene can define its own context-sensitive units, then perhaps object perception can only be described in terms of an unwieldy taxonomy of scenes and their unique perceptual units. One of the great accomplishments of the Gestaltists was to suggest a short list of rules for perceptual grouping that helped to organize many interesting examples. As is often the case in pioneering work, the rules were neither always obeyed nor exhaustive. No justification for the rules was given other than their evident plausibility. More seriously for practical applications, no effective computational algorithms were given to instantiate the rules. (p.142)

It should not go unmentioned, however, that Grossberg and Mingolla go on in this article to provide what they believe to be a step forward from the "scientific chaos" that they perceive as such a danger. Their model is based upon a set of analytic expressions that are collectively called the "Boundary Contour System Equations." In their 1985 paper, Grossberg and Mingolla do apply the model to a number of more or less well known perceptual phenomena with a substantial amount of success. These phenomena include certain textural discriminations (Beck, Prazdny, & Rosenfeld, 1983); the neon spreading illusion (Van Tuijl, 1975); the Glass Moire patterns (Glass & Switkes, 1976); and the Cafe Wall illusion (Gregory & Heard, 1979). In doing so, they have linked several visual phenomena to a common mechanism and may have taken a step forward from the "scientific chaos" they have viewed with such alarm.

However, Grossberg and Mingolla do stray from their goal of finding universal mechanisms in a way that suggests that they are still suffering along with the rest of us with the problem of idiosyncratic rules. In analyzing Beck's data, they point to a "remarkable aspect" of perceptual grouping due to colinearity. They ask "why do we continue to see a series of short lines if long lines are the emergent feature that control perceptual grouping?" (p. 150). Their response to this rhetorical question is to invoke at least two separate and distinct perceptual "outputs" from the boundary contrast system; one of which is terminator sensitive and one of which is not. Both, however, influence the perceptual outcome of the stimulus. This appears to me to be conceptually identical to the "multiple mechanisms solution" to the scientific chaos problems in visual psychology they have proposed elsewhere. The invocation of multiple mechanisms is conceptually identical to the invocation of multiple rules, from my point of view.

The situation seems the same even when we are dealing with as specific a problem as the search for a putative universal metric of visual space. How does the visual system distort or transform physical space as it views it with its "cyclopean eye"—an "eye" influenced by many monocular and dichoptic cues. Wagner (1985), in the very act of presenting a new metric for the transformations assayed by his experimental procedure, came to the conclusion:

> In sum, this multiplicity of well-supported theories indicates that no single geometry can adequately describe visual space under all conditions. Instead the geometry of visual space itself appears to be a function of stimulus conditions. (p. 493)

and I might add, of procedure as well.

Haig (1985) alludes to the same limitations on the search for generalities with regard to face recognition when he notes:

> Individual differences (in recognition strategy) are strong, however, and the variations are such that the uncritical application of generalized feature salience lists is neither useful nor appropriate. (p. 601)

Haig also goes on to explain that different stimulus faces seem to evoke different recognition strategies, thus further complicating the search for simple rules of face perception in particular and form perception in general.

It is possible that we simply do not yet perceive the grand scheme because our experiments have been too spotty and disorganized. The unfortunate conclusion is that whatever the youth of this science, the current state of affairs is one that points towards separation and independence of the constituent processes of perception. Whether this is to be its ultimate fate is yet to be determined. It should also be noted, lest one incorrectly concludes that the absence of general rules is unique to vision, that the underlying separateness of function seems also to be typical of many other psychological processes. Indeed, a recent report by Hammond, Hamm, and Grassia (1986) summed up the general problem in the following way:

> Doubts about the generality of results produced by psychological research have been expressed with increasing frequency since Koch (1959) observed, after a monumental review of scientific psychology in 1959, that there is "a stubborn refusal of psychological findings to yield to empirical generalization" (pp. 729-788). Brunswik (1952, 1956), Campbell and Stanley (1966), Cronbach (1975), Epstein (1979, 1980), Einhorn and Hogarth (1981), Greenwald (1975, 1976), Hammond (1966), Meehl (1978) and Simon (1979) among others, have also called attention to this situation. Jenkins (1974), warned that "a whole theory of an experiment can be elaborated without contributing in an important way to the science because the situation is artificial and *nonrepresentative*" [italics added] (p. 794). Tulving (1979) makes the startling observations that "after one hundred years of laboratory-based study of memory, we still do not seem to possess any concepts that the majority of workers would consider necessary or important." (p. 3)

Hammond, Hamm, and Grassia argue, comfortingly, that at least in the fields they have surveyed, this situation is caused not by the nature of human biology, but rather by the absence of an appropriate analytic methodology. They go on to suggest a technique that they believe would help to alleviate the lack of generality, and to apply that technique to a research problem in cognitive judgment. It is not possible for me to judge if their technique is suitable for the kind of perceptual separateness I have observed in my data, but that is not the purpose of this citation of the work of Hammond and his colleagues. My point is to demonstrate the ubiquity of this difficulty throughout psychology.

Many other distinguished psychologists have made the same point, including Ulric Neisser (1976). He also noted that the absence of generality and the limits of psychological facts to the specific experiments that originally produced them are ubiquitous properties of the field of cognitive psychology.

In sum, a considerable body of theoretical and empirical research, therefore, does seem currently to support the argument that the perceptual system is a constellation of relatively independent, and perhaps parallel, computational engines. Furthermore, analysis of a variety of cognitive theories also suggests that narrowness, specificity, and a lack of generality also characterizes work in that domain. (I am presently at work on another book in which I have made just such an analysis and feel strongly that this conclusion is valid there as well.)

We should make no mistake about this point: However abstract and esoteric it may seem, however remotely philosophical, the issue raised is fundamental. Have we missed the generalities (assuming they are there in some biological sense) because of the method of detail that we use for practical, paradigmatic reasons? Or, to the contrary, has our "hope" that these generalities exist blinded us to a very important, though contradictory, generality in its own right — namely, that there are few perceptual generalities, beyond the most global and truistic, to be discovered concerning visual perception?

The hope of providing some insight into this important controversy concerning the possible unification (as opposed to the ultimate separability) of visual perceptual processes, is one of the main motivations of the present study. Our chosen task is to seek out putative "rules" of visual perception in a context that is so structured and so constrained that the usual babble of the different paradigms, individual variations in performance, interobserver variation, and procedures would be muted. The plan is to study visual form perception in a situation that emphasizes the commonalities of procedure, task, observer, and stimulus-form such that the results are as comparable as possible. As we shall see, this is easier said than done for very practical considerations.

The vehicle for this research project is, as noted earlier, the dotted form — a "gracefully relaxed" abstraction of real visual scenes that is both computationally and psychophysically tractable. By psychophysically tractable, I refer to the ability of the stimulus material to serve in a wide variety of different visual tasks and to be manipulable at the preattentive level of processing on which I believe the perceptual transformations we are studying mainly lie. Ideally, the experiments carried out should be only minimally confounded by receptor or cognitive level effects that are extraneous to this intermediate level of visual form perception. By computationally tractable I refer to the fact that the stimulus-forms must also be simple enough to be amenable to formal mathematical or computer analysis and modeling. Arrays of dots, discrete samples of continuous forms, meet this criterion, whereas much more complex and all-too-complete photographic images (for example, of real world scenes) usually do not. A modern graphics computer is capable of processing a 64 or 100 dot pattern in three dimensions in a few seconds or minutes, whereas it would bog down hopelessly in a computational explosion should the billion or so pixels of a three-dimensional volume (a thoroughly plausible possibility considering that volumes can be sampled as densely as the currently standard 1000 × 1000 pixel graphics display image and be a thousand deep as well) be submitted to it for processing.

Dotted images have many other advantages. The visibility (in the broadest sense of the term) of the forms the dots are sampling can be continuously regulated by embedding an ordered dotted form in an array of randomly distributed dots. This provides a means of degrading a stimulus in a precise manner so that the powerful information processing ability of the visual system can be challenged. It is an unavoidable fact that in many less demanding signal-to-noise situations the visual system performs so well and is so adaptive that it is difficult to tease out any differential effects of form, per se.

A related advantage of the masked, dotted forms used here, is that, like the random dot stereograms of which they are a subset that were introduced into visual research by Bela Julesz (1960), they reduce extraneous (i.e., irrelevant to the purposes of the experiment) cues to a minimum and allow the study of a pure form of visual perception unconfounded by redundant cues that would "give away the game" without challenging the visual task of interest. In other words, dotted stimulus-forms reduce the number of redundant cues to a minimum, if not to a single one ("arrangement?"), and allow one to test what one intends to test rather than inadvertently providing a multi-cue stimulus-scenes to the ever opportunistic, powerful, and multiply sensitive visual system.

Another important attribute of dotted forms is that because the *organization* of the "trivial" constituent dots is everything as far as the perceiver is concerned, they allow the experimenter to specifically explore the effect of overall arrangement and global form and to minimize the influence of local features. There are, in fact, no local "features" in a dotted form, only the minimum amount of information necessary to define the location of the dot—all else is nothing more than a manifestation of the organization and spatial interrelationships between and among the dots. Since the human visual system, as the Gestaltists would have taught us if we had been listening, sees more by virtue of the *arrangement of the parts* and less by means of the *nature of the parts,* this seems to me to be a particularly appropriate means of exploring global form perception. Modern support for this primacy of globality can be found in the work of Navon (1977) among others. However, a substantial body of data also supports the opposite view. And, indeed, it probably is the case that more students of the field are currently local feature types than are globalists. The reader is directed to the work of Anne Triesman and her colleagues (Triesman, Skyes, & Gelade, 1977; Triesman & Gelade, 1980; Triesman & Schmidt 1982; Triesman & Patterson, 1984; and Triesman & Souther, 1986) for a strong counterargument in favor of local feature precedence. It is also the case nowadays, however, that we are beginning to appreciate that there are different situations in which global and local properties dominate respectively. The point is forcefully made by Goldmeier's (1936/1972) and Klein and Barresi's (1985) recent expansion of his work.

Another important advantage of dotted forms, particularly in the present context in which we wish to compare performance in a number of different tasks, is that virtually the same stimulus materials — the to-be-perceived forms and the interfering masks — can be used unchanged in each of the experimental conditions without contamination by experience or memory. Indeed, it is possible to make comparisons between detection (is there anything there?), discrimination (are those two things the same or different?), and recognition (what is the name of that thing?) using only slightly different methodologies and apparatuses, the same stimuli, and, as we shall see, even in some instances the same observers. Because the stimuli are degraded in exactly the same way — the signal-to-noise ratio is varied by adding greater or lesser numbers of randomly positioned noise dots — direct comparisons can be made between relative performance levels and qualitative sensitivities in each of the three tasks.

In the past our work on masked dotted form perception primarily has been concerned with detection, first of two dimensional stimulus-forms (Uttal, 1975), then of planar surfaces in three-dimensional space (Uttal, 1983), and then of nonplanar surfaces in three-dimensional space (Uttal, 1984). A few rules of visual perception emerged in this work that characterized particular situations. Later, I summarize these rules, but for the moment the important point is that the rules observed in one context often did not generalize to other, at first glance analogous, experimental conditions in spite of the unusually good control to which I just alluded. This is the message of the metarule presented earlier. What held true in two-dimensions does not necessarily hold in three-dimensions; and what held for regular forms does not always hold for random forms. As I have already noted, specificity of process, rather than generality, was the rule of rules. In some cases the discrepancy between conditions was not only surprising, but downright astonishing, and certainly counterintuitive.

Specifically, two rules[2] emerged from our earlier studies that, from some points of view, must have seemed to be inconsistent with each other. Yet each was so well founded empirically that they could not be dismissed as arti-

---

[2]In my earlier work I also hypothesized the existence of a third rule — The rule of random sampling. This rule summarized the findings of a number of experiments arguing strongly that randomly sampled surfaces were detected better than regularly sampled surfaces. On the basis of extensive replications of that work, I now must recant on that rule. It appears that the results were spurious, possibly based on individual differences in different samples of observers, but whatever the cause, incorrect. My recantation is spelled out in more complete detail in Appendix A of this book.

factual or the superficial outcome of differing procedures or individual differences. These rules are:

1. *The rule of linear periodicity.* This rule emerged from the two-dimensional work (Uttal, 1975). It summarized much of the detection work that had been carried out in that domain by asserting that evenly spaced (periodic, in our terminology) straight lines of dots were the prepotent stimulus for two-dimensional detection. This rule was predicted and, to a certain degree, even explained by a two-dimensional autocorrelation transformation (Uttal, 1975)

2. *The rule of three-dimensional noncomputability.* This rule reflected the empirical fact that the three-dimensional form had little or no effect on nonplanar stimulus detectability. Even though form in two dimensions had been a powerful determinant of detectability, our observers seemed to be insensitive to the three-dimensional shape (i.e., the depth parameters) of the stimulus. This was so in spite of the fact that the solid *appearance* of the stimulus-forms was striking when they were viewed through the stereoscope. Unlike the first rule, this phenomenon remains to this time theoretically unexplained, but as we shall see later in this monograph, it, too, is often idiosyncratic and violated in what are only slightly different experimental paradigms involving alternative tasks.

Measures of form effects were always the most inconsistent and labile outcome of our experiments. Intersubject differences were the greatest when data were analyzed for this variable. The number of different stimulus-forms in the experimental set, the experimental tasks, and many other variables of an experiment seemed to produce wide variation in answers to the question — What is the effect of stimulus-form on detection, discrimination, and recognition? Indeed, at present, we cannot answer this question with any degree of conviction.

As we shall also see, it was only when a different kind of analysis — confusion error matrices — was introduced (i.e., other than plotting our raw percentage-correct scores as a function of form) that stable effects of form emerged). These matrices show relatively reliable and stable confusions and although this is an unexpected kind of differential performance as a function of form, the question we sought to answer originally, it is a form effect. It is possible that in some way we do not yet understand, the use of sets of different forms taps into processes that are more active or cognitive than they are passive and preattentive. Of this, possibility I have more to say later.

It should be noted that others may not feel as I do that the data concerning the absence of form effects are yet unexplained. In particular, Stevens (1986) reviewing one of the earlier books in this series (Uttal, 1984) in which this conjecture was originally presented, suggests that the rule of three-dimensional noncomputability is, in fact, predicted by the theoretical work of

Grimson (1981), Marr (1982), and Mayhew (1982), some of the leaders in computational vision. Stevens' argument is that all of them *"regard stereopsis to occur "in the image plane"* [his quotes] *as it were, by matching corresponding tokens in the two images according to the ordering, continuity, and other constraints . . . "* (p. 24).

It is, unfortunately, not clear just how Stevens comes to this conclusion. Marr's well-known theory is based upon a sequential series of processing steps that include the calculation of the primal sketch, the raw and full 2 1/2-dimension sketches, and then, finally, the full 3-dimension representation. The transformation of the two retinal images into the full stereoscopic image, however, is not a single process that can be properly said to be occurring "in the image plane" or, for that matter, at any other level of this multilevel transformation. Rather, the two-dimensional "image plane" information is but the raw material that is fed into the sequence of processes that eventually produces the neurally encoded (or computer simulated) perceptual experience of depth. The raw input to the system guides and defines, but it is not the stuff of the perceptual experience. To say otherwise, if I may draw an analogy by generating a reductio ad absurdum, would be to suggest that the perception of color takes place in the electromagnetic spectrum! Thus, I do not believe that the mathematical models to which Stevens alludes adequately explain this still surprising result.[3]

Furthermore, it must not be overlooked that the distribution of the random noise dots throughout a stereoscopically generated volume *does* decrease their effectiveness as masks, by virtue of their being subjectively dedensified even if the nonplanar stimulus forms are not so "subjectively dedensified." If "stereopsis took place in the image plane," then this effect of noise dedensification would become equally as perplexing and difficult to explain as is the absence of the signal dedensification.

Perhaps the main difficulty with Steven's original argument is engendered by different attributed meanings of the word "stereopsis." To a psychologist, and I may add, as well as to the general public who publish conventional dictionaries, stereopsis is the *perception of a form in three-dimensions.* It is not the *process of a generating that form,* but rather the outcome of the computations. I believe this is also the meaning that Marr (1982) attributes to the word, although he finesses a precise definition of the word in both his glossary and his text. What he does do is to very carefully distinguish between *disparity* as a stimulus cue to depth and *depth* as the psychological experience, and, this I believe, is equivalent to the distinction I make (but Stevens does not) between stereopsis — the three-dimensional percept — and its coded rep-

---

[3]In recent correspondence with him, Stevens indicates that he now agrees with the point of view that I express here.

resentation in the "image plane" — the two-dimensional proximal stimuli on the retina.

Stevens confuses, from my point of view, the perceptual experience and the mathematical or neural transformation process that leads to that experience. Stereopsis is certainly a three-dimensional construct formed out of two-dimensional stimulus information, but it is not clear how this could be construed to mean that "stereopsis occurs in the image plane" or how that vague concept could explain these data.

Thus, the problem remaining is: Why does the behavior of the observer in this psychophysical experiment not follow the dimensions of the perceptual experience (reduced subjective density of the stimulus-form engendered by the disparity differences introduced by experimenter into the stimuli does not reduce detectability) even though subjective dedensification does influence masking effects in seemingly similar situations (e.g., decreased subjective density of the random masking dots due to the same kind of disparity differences does lead to an increase in detection performance)? It is as if the information contained in the two two-dimensional retina images is preserved in some way so that even though we perceive the three-dimensional outcome of the transformation from two-dimensions, under certain conditions we can tap into some residual trace of the original planar stimulus as it existed prior to that transformation. These words, however, are not a satisfying and complete explanation any more than is the phrase "stereopsis occurs in the image plane."

The logic of the situation has been elucidated by Daugman (1984). In one of those seminal papers that serve as milestones of current progress and guideposts to future accomplishments in any field, he has shown that it is necessary to think of visual space as a two-dimensional phenomenon. Although his argument is that the (generally) one-dimensional theories and experiments (using gratings as stimuli) are inadequate to represent the results of what is essentially a two-dimensional problem, one can also look at the problem from the point of view of the relationship between the two-dimensional stimulus and the three-dimensional stereoscopic experience. It may be that this is the point that Stevens wishes to make — that there is some residual trace of two-dimensionality in three-dimensional vision and this is certainly what our experiments seem to suggest, but the nature of that residual information and the constraints on stereopsis are yet to be described.

At this point it becomes clear that the perceptual universe assayed by this dotted stimulus-form-in-dotted-noise experimental paradigm and the visual processes that are being invoked are much more complex and the forthcoming results are much less generalizable than I had initially hoped. The nature of the domain of this perceptual universe also began to take on a more concrete and specific form as indicated in Figure 1. This diagrammatic chart illu-

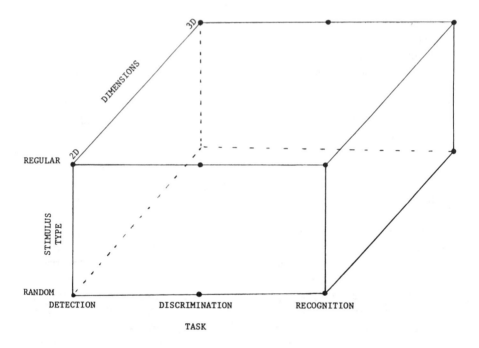

FIG. 1    The experimental space in which this program of research has been carried out defined by the three major independent variables — the number of dimensions, the stimulus type, and the task.

strates the 12 conditions of the experiments that we have carried out and the three dimensions that have been explored. The three independent variable dimensions that we have compared are random and regular stimuli, two- and three-dimensional stimulus-forms, and three different tasks.

The issue of a unified theory as opposed to a "grab bag of perceptual tricks" remains persistent and perplexing in even this little corner of perceptual psychophysics. But it is not the only controversial problem attacked in this study. Another persistent problem at this intermediate, postreceptor, but preattentive level of visual perception concerns whether or not the detection, discrimination, recognition, and any other related visual processes yet to be encountered operate in parallel (concurrently) or in serial (sequentially). This is an issue that has attracted widespread attention in recent years, particularly as the concept of parallel processing evolved in both computer science and in neuroscience. Indeed, some recent neuroanatomical and neurophysiological evidence is beginning to accumulate that supports parallelism. Kas (1982), for example, has demonstrated a wide variety of brain regions in the squirrel monkey that seem to execute separate visual functions. This datum provides an anatomical basis for the concept of perceptually separate functions. In related work, Zeki (1978, 1983) has studied the organization of the brain of monkeys and has shown that different areas also are responsive to specific features of a stimulus such as color, movement, and orientation, among others. Though this separation of feature-triggered sensitivity in neurons is not exactly the same thing as the separation of functions evidenced in Kas' work, it does illustrate a dispersion and parallel localization of function to cortical regions that fits well with the idea that different tasks may also be mediated by separate regions and mechanisms and thus have distinctive properties.

Recent work, however, suggests that the differentiation of function of the many visual cortical areas may be quite unlike the scheme proposed by Zeki. Van Essen (1985) reports that virtually all of these areas are responsive to several different kinds of stimulus attributes such as color, motion, form, and depth. He has no doubt that there are measurable differences in the characteristics of the receptive field of the various regions, but no area seems to be totally unresponsive to any of these stimulus attributes.

There is even some physiological evidence from studies of brain responses in humans that speaks to the concurrence versus sequentiality issue. Parasuraman and Beatty (1980) report the presence of two distinct evoked brain potential waveforms that seem to separately reflect detection (N100) and recognition (P300) at the indicated millisecond delay following the stimulus. The fact that one wave occurs after the other suggests that they do not work in parallel even though their findings do not allow us to say anything about the localization of the processes.

Theoretical attacks (e.g., Nolte, 1967; Starr, Metz, Lusted, & Goodenough, 1975) on the problem have offered arguments supporting the notion of concurrent and parallel, though separate, mechanisms, possibly with very comparable information thresholds for their activation. Other experimental psychophysical work (e.g., Swets, Green, Getty, & Swets, 1978; Sagi & Julesz, 1985) also supports this point of view.

An alternative conceptual solution to the question of serial versus parallel organization deals with vision as a series of sequential stages or levels of information processing with which successively more complex transformations and decisions are made and at which progressively more information is required. One intuitively attractive hypothesis of this genre relevant to the present study is that the human observer first *detects* forms on the basis of a minimum amount of information, then is able to *discriminate* two detected stimuli from each other as slightly more information becomes available, and subsequently *recognizes* or identifies the stimulus-form when sufficient amounts of information are available.

Implicit in such a hypothetical system is the concept that at each of these three levels of visual processing, successively higher amounts of information must be extracted by the observer to be utilized. Said another way, the performance on some of the successive visual information processing tasks must be accomplished before the other tasks can be initiated. One nonintuitive counterargument to such a hypothesis lies in some relatively rare data obtained from well-controlled comparisons of detection, discrimination, and recognition behavior. Furcher, Thomas, and Campbell (1977), for example, have reported that the difference between detection and what they refer to as "discrimination thresholds" of spatial frequency varying grating-type stimuli were in most cases accounted for if simple probability and harmonic summation considerations were taken into account. Their suggestion, therefore, is that there is no processing hierarchy—both thresholds are achieved at the same information levels at least for this particular kind of stimulus. Other workers have reported this same phenomenon in other contexts—a surprisingly small difference between the detection and discrimination theresholds. It is as if any observer can distinguish *what* is there virtually as soon as he can distinguish *that* something is there.

Even more interesting and counterintuitive, however, in some situations the performance of the observer may run counter to the predictions of the hierarchical model of information acquisition in an even more astonishing manner. Several workers (Diener, 1981; Doehrman, 1974) have reported that under certain circumstances recognition performance can actually be more accurate than detection performance at the same stimulus information levels. At first glance such a result would imply that the observer is able to recognize something that he cannot detect, a result that is obviously contrary to the hierarchical information acquisition theory. This result suggests that the two tasks are mediated by the same processes and raises the possibility of a paradoxical world in which form identification might even exist in the absence of detection.

However, the actual nonmysterious nature of the possibility of equal detection and recognition, or even the superiority of the latter over the former, has been clarified by Green and Birdsall (1978), who evaluated several alternative models. At least one—the disjunctive model—predicts that recognition and detection performance levels should be very close. A specific explanation of the apparent superiority of recognition over detection is presented by Thomas, Gille, and Barker (1982). They point out, in analyzing an experiment in which either one of two alternative gratings could be present in one of two sequential presentations (the 2 × 2 experimental design that is frequently used in this type of investigation), that it might be possible for an observer to use information from both presentations (e.g., "nothing present" in a spatial subregion of either the stimulus or stimulus plus noise presentation may be useful information) to correctly identify a stimulus even when detection was not possible. This sort of process could, according to them, be framed in the context of a low threshold theoretical explanation of the visual process in contrast to a high threshold explanation, which would preclude identification without detection.

What at first glance must seem to be paradoxical results and, thus, curious conclusions makes this issue worthy of considerable further attention. This is particularly true because most of the studies that have been concerned with this problem, particularly in recent years, have used grating-type stimuli to explore this problem. However, accumulating evidence (for example, Coffin, 1978) indicates that this approach does not generalize to other stimulus types and, therefore, it is not certain that any data speaking to this form of a hierarchical or unitary visual processing model would be more broadly applicable. It is important, therefore, to determine if we can generalize the conclusions drawn with gratings to other types of stimulus materials.

As noted, a major purpose of present study is to explore the effect of three-dimensional form on detection, discrimination, and recognition. In some of our earlier work (Uttal, 1984), as summarized by the rule of three-dimensional noncomputability, it was observed that the stereoscopically generated, three-dimensional geometry of a stimulus-form did not affect its detectability. This results suggests that even though the human visual system is capable of easily perceiving three-dimensional form (specifically depth) it is not necessarily capable of coping with the enormous information processing requirements of all kinds of three-dimensional perceptual processes.

The failure to totally process disparity-generated apparent depth serves as one measure of the limits of the preattentive aspects of human visual perception. Support that such a limit is real and not a procedural artifact, and that there are real differences between two-dimensional and three-dimensional perception, has recently come from the work of Julesz and Chang (1984), Lappin, Langston, and Livert (1984), and Northdurft (1985), all of whom have shown a breakdown of certain other aspects of multi-dimensional perception when the visual domain of an experiment is moved from the plane to stereoscopically generated solids. In Julesz' and Chang's case, as well as in that of Northdurft, the breakdown of the texton hypothesis (originally proposed in Julesz, 1981) was observed, and in that of Lappin and his colleagues, orientation sensitivity in two dimensions disappeared when the experimental paradigm was shifted to three dimensions. Another specific purpose of the present study, therefore, is to determine if the reported insensitivity to the three-dimensional shape of an object also obtains in the discriminability and recognition tasks. As we shall see, recognition, contrary to the results forthcoming from the detection and discrimination experiments, does, in fact, seem to be sensitive in complex ways to the geometrical form of the stimulus in the raw percent correct data. However, this effect is idiosyncratic. It is only when we dig deeply into the discrimination and recognition data — specifically the error matrices — that these data display stable form effects.

This study also adds comparisons of the discriminability and recognizability of regular and random forms to the comparable results for detection. As we have seen, and as I report in more detail in Appendix A, the results for similar experiments in detection have been equivocal and I do not believe the validity of my earlier findings that randomly sampled stimuli are detected better than regularly sampled stimuli. In spite of the fact that this type of experiment is known to be confounded — there is a monocularly visible straight line cue present in the regular stimuli — it still seems worthwhile to determine how our observers deal with this variable. The advantage given to the regular stimuli by the additional monocularly perceived straight lines of dots makes it impossible to independently evaluate the influence of this variable, however.

# 2 Background[4]

The dot-masking paradigm has proven over the years to be a rich source of data and ideas related to problems of form perception. The research reported in this monograph is the outgrowth and continuation of over a decade of research in this laboratory mainly reported in three monographs — Uttal, 1975; 1983; 1984 and in a series of separate papers cited there.

The purity[5] of the dotted stimulus-forms used in this study (that is, their relative freedom from both energy-driven receptor influences and context-dependent semantic and cognitive influences) allows us to examine some subtle, intermediate level, information-processing attributes of vision that would have been hidden or overwhelmed by either energy-sensitive, peripheral mechanisms (if dim, low-contrast stimuli had been used) or by meaning-dominated, central effects (if non-dotted, natural, or realistic scenes had been used). In short, what is virtually an ideal method for studying a particular kind of preattentive geometrical and spatio-temporal organizational influence on an intermediate level of form vision has been chosen for this study. However, this power does not come without cost. This dotted, discrete, sampled domain, as I noted in Chapter 1, is the only context to which the results of this work are directly relevant; the results are not necessarily

---

[4]Some of the material in this chapter has been adapted from my earlier monographs (Uttal, 1975; 1983; 1984) in a revised and expanded form.

[5]It is interesting to note that the abstraction — dotted forms in dotted noise — that we use as a model reality in these experiments has many real analogs. For example, Goldmeier (1965) noted long ago that reading radiographs of carcinomas posed exactly the same kind of dotted signal-in-dotted noise task that is used in this study as a probe to define the rules of visual perception.

germane nor can they be uncritically transferred to describe either more peripheral or more central levels of visual information processing or continuous stimuli unless independently validated by the appropriate experimental tests.

Theoretically, our approach to theory testing has depended largely upon the continuous mathematics familiar to workers in the field of computer image processing. Originally, a straightforward two-dimensional autocorrelation was used to model the results of two-dimensional detection tasks. This model was very successful (Uttal, 1975) and, I believe, gave an unusually deep insight into the perceptual forces at work in that domain. However, when the focus of this work was moved to three-dimensional stimulus-forms, simple autocorrelation ideas no longer worked: The model predicted behavior (e.g., sensitivity to the stereoscopically generated apparent depth) that was not obtained in the psychophysical experiments. While there was an exquisite sensitivity to density changes in the $x$ and $y$ dimensions, no such effect occurred when stimulus forms were stretched in depth by stereoscopic procedures.

Contrary to an earlier conclusion drawn by me in Uttal (1983), therefore, it seems that the three perceived spatial dimensions — the $x$ and $y$ dimensions that are isomorphically related to the retinal image and the $z$ dimension that must be inferred, computed, or constructed from the invariances in the two retinal images — are *not* processed in exactly the same way. This conclusion is further enhanced by an important corollary experiment carried out by Wilfred Kincaid of the University of Michigan and myself that is reported later in this monograph.

In spite of the fact that it did not generalize in all regards to three-dimensions, the two-dimensional model is instructive in preparing us for later discussion in which other models are invoked to explain the data obtained in the present study. As we shall see in Chapter 5, the two-dimensional model does not extrapolate simply to the three-dimensional case because of some surprising limitations of the visual system (e.g., the *apparent* density of a stimulus form does not affect detectability or discrimination as predicted even though that of the masking dots does.)

The autocorrelation transformation used in our two-dimensional model is based on the following formula:

$$A_c(\Delta x, \Delta y) = \int \int f(x,y) \cdot f(x + \Delta x, y + \Delta y) dy\, dx \qquad \text{(Eq. 1)}$$

where $\Delta x$ and $\Delta y$ are shifts in the positions of a two-dimensional stimulus-form, $f(x,y)$ required to produce a shifted replica $f(x + \Delta x, y + \Delta y)$. The shifted replica and the original form are then compared with each other by cross multiplication and the values of these cross products are then integrated across all positions in the space. When two two-dimensional forms (i.e., the original and shifted forms) are compared in this way, the result is a three-dimensional graph in the $\Delta x$, $\Delta y$ space — a value of $(\Delta x, \Delta y)$ is generated indicating the intersections of the dots of $f(x, y)$ and $f(x + \Delta x, y + \Delta y)$ for all possible shifted positions. It is interesting to note that the auto — or for that matter — the cross correlations of two three-dimensional patterns produce a four-dimensional output (that is, a value of $A(\Delta x, \Delta y, \Delta z)$ for all shifted positions in the three-dimensional $(\Delta x, \Delta y, \Delta z)$ space as the forms are shifted by each other.

A family of $A(\Delta x, \Delta y)$ values were thus computed for all possible $\Delta x$ and $\Delta y$ combinations to fill the three-dimensional $(A, \Delta x, \Delta y)$ space that is generated when a two-dimensional space is autocorrelated. Samples of two simulated stimuli that can serve as inputs to the autocorrelation processor and two photographs of the computer plot of their discrete autocorrelated outputs are shown in Figure 2. The first plate in this figure shows a straight dotted-line stimulus and is autocorrelation. The second plate shows the same dotted-line embedded in random masking-dots; it should be noted that the peaks in the autocorrelation space most closely associated with the straight-line of dots

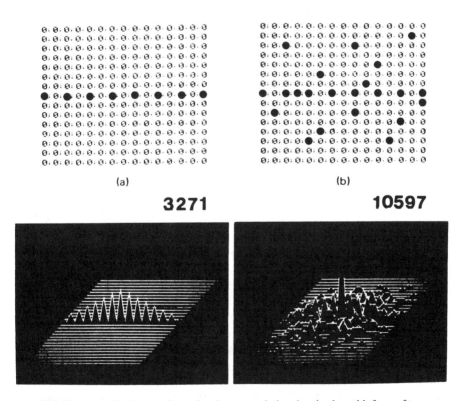

(a)                    (b)

3271                10597

FIG. 2    A sample of a two-dimensional autocorrelation showing how this form of transformation could account for the two-dimensional results reported in Uttal (1975).

are higher than other peaks. This is a clue as to how this mechanism might be used to discriminate a periodic line of dots from random dots in either the brain or the computer: Form has been converted into amplitude and the highest peaks are mainly associated with the most periodic lines of dots. Of course, it is not this simple for other nonlinear or three-dimensional forms, but similar transformational cues may also apply when orderly forms must be extracted in such cases.

The two-dimensional autocorrelational surface is made up of a number of peaks of varying amplitudes distributed in the $\Delta x$, $\Delta y$ space.

By applying the following empirical expression:

$$F_m = \frac{\sum\limits_{n=1}^{N} \sum\limits_{i=1}^{N} (A_n \times A_i)/d_{ni}}{N} \; ; n \neq i \qquad \text{(Eq. 2)}$$

a single numerical "Figure of Merit" ($F_m$) for detection can be generated for each autocorrelated stimulus pattern. In this expression, $A_i$ and $A_n$ are the amplitudes of peaks taken pairwise, $D$ is the Pythagorean distance in the $\Delta x$, $\Delta y$ space between the two peaks, and $N$ is the number of peaks. The purely arbitrary and ad hoc expression produces families of $F_m$'s that are closely associated with the relative psychophysical detectability of sets of two-dimensional stimulus forms. This expression for the *detection* of two-dimensional forms does not, however, predict performance in the three-dimensional detection case and probably does not work for two-dimensional discrimination and recognition, although we have never run the relevant experiments to test this hypothesis.

The three-dimensional analog of this transform is conceptually identical. It is quite simply extrapolated from the two-dimensional version by adding the third level of integration as depicted in the following formula.

$$A_c(\Delta x, \Delta y, \Delta z) = \int\int\int f(x,y,z) \cdot f(x+\Delta x, y+\Delta, z+\Delta z)\,dx\,dy\,dz \qquad \text{(Eq. 3)}$$

Though conceptually quite similar to the two-dimensional model discussed earlier, the addition of the third dimension adds a substantial computational load and it has been necessary both to use a more powerful computer than previously (an Apollo 660 as opposed to a Cromemco S/3) and to be more patient: Even with the new and significantly more powerful processor, computation time went from a few seconds for the two-dimensional transforms to 20 to 25 minutes for the three-dimensional ones. This is brief enough to allow computer experiments to be carried out whereas the twelve hour computation time that was required when we tried to carry out the same calculations on the Cromemco computer was not.

Even greater processing advantages (e.g., the processing time could be reduced to two to three minutes per three-dimensional autocorrelation) have subsequently been achieved by using forward and inverse Fast Fourier transformations to implement the correlation transformations. This is possible because of the interchangability of the correlation and Fourier transformations and the fast techniques that have been specifically developed for the Fourier transform. This technique was introduced into this laboratory by Mr. Ramakrishna Kakarala, an outstanding computer science student from the University of Michigan who spent the summers of 1985 and 1986 in the NOSC-Hawaii Laboratory after a very successful semester working in Ann Arbor. Specifically, Kakarala based his algorithm on the fact that the autocorrelation $A_c(\Delta x, \Delta y)$ of a function $f(x,y)$ is equal to the inverse Fast Fourier Transform (FFT) of the product of the forward FFT of $f(x,y)$ times the complex conjugate of the FFT of f$(x,y)$. That is:

$$A_c(\Delta x, \Delta y) = \text{FFT}^{-1} (\text{FFT} \{f(x,y)\} \, x \, \text{FFT}^* \{f(x,y)\}) \qquad \text{(Eq. 4)}$$

Similarly, the cross correlation can be defined as:

$$C_c(\Delta x, \Delta y) = \text{FFT}^{-1} (\text{FFT} \{f_1(x,y)\} \, x \, \text{FFT}^* \{f_2(x,y)\}) \qquad \text{(Eq. 5)}$$

Although there are some constraints on these approximations and the stimuli must artificially be made periodic, the discrete versions of the transformation do reproduce the auto-and cross-correlation of dotted forms exactly.

Although these formulae are presented here in terms of the integral calculus and in the terminology of infinitesimals, in our actual model the transformations were originally implemented on the computer in the form of a discrete approximation to these integral equations. A complete description of the discrete algorithm actually used to compute the two-dimensional autocorrelation has been presented in Uttal (1975) and it is conceptually identical to the three-dimensional case. The following discussion concentrates on the two-dimensional case for clarity but it is a direct and straight-forward extrapolation to the higher dimension.

One obstacle to continued progress on this problem is, as I have mentioned, that psychophysical processes in three-dimensions do not exhibit the orderliness of analogous processes in two dimensions. The remainder of this chapter describes some of the discontinuities, unpredicted performance, and surprises that occurred when we moved from the relatively simple two-dimensional case to the perceptually much more demanding three-dimensional one. The additional computing load seemed to have been too much for the brain to handle, and extrapolations of the simple models no longer were adequate, therefore, to describe our observers' behavior.

In the two-dimensional detection case, this simple figure of merit worked well, indeed, in predicting the following results. In the first of the three previous monographs (Uttal, 1975) the effects of variations on form detectability of a number of different attributes of two-dimensional stimulus-forms were evaluated in a series of psychophysical experiments using two-dimensional visual masks. Specifically, I considered the effects of each of the following attributes and found the results indicated for each of the following dimensions:

1. The larger the number of dots in a form, the more detectable was the form.
2. Line orientation had no effect on detectability.
3. The deformation of straight-lines into curves and angles made the resulting stimulus-forms less detectable than the original straight lines.
4. Colinear dot-spacing irregularity was important; the more irregular the line of dots, the less detectable it became.
5. Transverse dot-spacing irregularity had the same effect. The more irregular the line, the less detectable.
6. If parts were deleted from triangles, deletion of the sides was more effective in reducing detectability than were the corners. The perception of triangularity depended more on the lines of the sides than on the corners. This is probably a corrolary of 3.
7. The orientation of polygons had no effect on their detectability.
8. If squares were distorted into parallelograms, the greater the distortion, the less detectable were the stimulus forms.
9. Organized straight-line patterns were more detectable than "pick-up-sticks" patterns composed of exactly the same lines.
10. If one distorted squares and triangles by misplacing one or more corners, the greater the distortion, the less detectable were the stimulus forms.
11. The degree of figural goodness had no effect on detectability.

The order of detectability of the forms in each of the psychophysical experiments was compared with the order of the figures of merit generated from the autocorrelated transforms of the stimulated stimulus-forms. In most cases, the two rank orders were in agreement. There were, however, some discrepancies between the two rank orders. A few forms that showed differences in their respective figures of merit in the simulation produced no comparable differences in psychophysical performance. Furthermore, while the figure of merit for forms that varied in "figural goodness" were in substantial agreement with the psychophysical data, there were some particular cases in which order reversals appeared. These discrepancies seemed to be mainly due to a lack of sensitivity on the part of the autocorrelation model to forms that possessed preponderantly diagonal arrangements of the constituent dots. Some of these discrepancies between theory and psychophysical findings, were probably due to deficiencies in the formulation of the empirical figure of merit expression but others may have more to do with the linear and Cartesian nature of the coordinate system in which the transformations were made. Polar coordinate transformations have repeatedly been suggested to me as an alternative strategy.

In the second series of experiments, reported in Uttal (1983), I turned from two-dimensional stimuli hidden in two-dimensional masks to stimuli that, while still two-dimensional themselves (single dots, lines, and planes), were embedded among random visual masking-dots that were arrayed in three-dimensional space. This work produced a number of results that have added to our understanding of how dotted forms are perceived.

1. As an unmitigated generality, increasing the number of masking-dots monotonically reduced the detectability of a dotted stimulus-form when all other variables are held constant. Similarly, decreasing the number of dots in the stimulus-form decreased its detectability. In other words, the raw signal (stimulus-dot numerosity) -to-noise (masking-dot numerosity) ratio was a powerful determinant of dotted-form detection. Although not surprising, this outcome is an important cross-referencing parameter, as we shall see in experiments 1, 2, and 3 in the present work, as well as being of interest in its own right. This outcome confirmed and extended the findings concerning signal-to-noise ratios from the earier study (Uttal, 1975) with two-dimensional stimuli. (However, as we shall see later, even though decreasing the *apparent* dot density in the mask by stretching it over space in three dimensions did increase detectability, decreasing the *apparent* density of the stimulus-form in a similar way did not reduce it detectability.)

2. The position of a repetitive flashing dot in the apparent cubical space exerted only a minor effect on its detectability. A dot placed far off the rear, lower, right-hand corner was seen slightly less well than dots at other positions, and one centered in space was seen slightly better. Although I presented no equivalent data concerning the translations of lines or planes, within similar limits and on the basis of my two-dimensional results, I believe this result also holds for such multi-dimensional stimuli.

3. Repetitively flashed dots with interdot intervals of 100 msec were seen better than those with shorter or longer intervals when the number of flashed dots was held constant. The function relating single-dot detectability to interdot interval was thus nonmonotonic and suggests the existence of an optimum interval of about this duration.

4. In dotted-form discrimination, there was a substantial advantage gained by using a dichoptic viewing condition that allowed the perceptual construction of depth compared to either binocular or monocular viewing conditions in which no disparity cue to depth was present. Somewhat surprisingly, on the other hand, binocular viewing produced somewhat higher detection scores than did monocular viewing, in spite of the fact that there was no informational difference between the stimuli in these two nondisparity viewing conditions.

5. Increasing the temporal interdot interval between sequential dots in a straight line of dots led to a monotonic and nearly linear reduction in the detectability of the line. It is unclear whether this was due to the increase in the time interval per se or to the increased number of masking-dots encompassed by the longer duration of the dot train. What is certain is that apparent movement did not substitute in any way for simultaneity.

6. Very surprisingly, irregularity of the temporal intervals between the plotting of successive dots did not appreciably diminish dotted-line detection. A high degree of interdot-interval irregularity could be tolerated without reduction in detection scores.

7. Spatial irregularity of the dots along a straight line affected detectability at short interdot-intervals (less than or equal to 30 msec). However, at longer dot intervals these same spatial irregularities exerted little influence on detectability. In some manner, visual mechanisms seemed to be able to compensate for these spatial distortions if sufficient time elapsed between the plotting of sequential dots.

8. An increase in the disorder of the sequence in which a series of regularly spaced (in time and position) lines of dots was plotted produced only a modest, though monotonic, decrease in the detectability of the form. This form of irregularity, so extreme that it violated the spatio-temporal topology of the stimulus-form, could still be partially overcome, presumably by the same mechanisms that were capable of "smoothing" temporal and spatial irregularity.

9. Dotted-line orientation in space was ineffective in influencing detectability scores. Visual space was isotropic for diagonal lines.

10. When two planes were to be discriminated from each other with regard to their respective depths:

a.   The greater the dichoptic disparity between the two planes, the more easily one was discriminated from the other.

b.   The effect of the number of dots in the two planes was relatively small. Indeed, discrimination of a highly reduced stimulus consisting of only two dots was easily accomplished.

c.   A reduction in viewing time led to a progressive though modest reduction in the discrimination of the two planes.

d.   When a burst of masking-dots followed the presentation of a dichoptic stimulus, stereoscopic performance was especially degraded at intervals less than 50 msec. This is probably a good measure of the time it takes for stereopsis to develop.

11. The form of a planar stimulus composed of even a relatively large number of randomly arrayed dots had a suprisingly small effect on its detectability, given what we had previously learned in the earlier two-dimensional studies with dotted-outline forms. Even when the viewing time was reduced, further impoverishing the dot-masked stimulus, form defined

in this way remained an ineffective variable and any putative effect of shape was not enhanced. Furthermore, the effect of even as drastic a manipulation as changing the stimulus-form from a square to an elongated rectangle was slight. On the other hand, this conclusion did not hold for forms defined by dotted-outlines. Dotted-outline forms showed a strong increase in detectability as they became more oblong. This seemed to be accounted for by the detectability of the constituent line rather than the forms of which they were constituent parts. The "prepotency of the part" observed in this situation was confirmed later in a study (Yu, Brogan, Robertson, & Uttal, 1985) in which it was shown that individual strokes of dotted approximations to chinese characters were as detectable as the entire characters.

12.  There was virtually no effect on detectability when a planar stimulus-form defined by a random array of dots was rotated around the y axis. When the form was rotated in more complex ways around two or three axes the experiment outcome was equally unaffected. This effect was confirmed for more elaborate, elastic, planar stimuli by Kincaid and Uttal (1986), and is reported here in experiment 7.

13.  The gradient of form detectability was very steep between 88 and 90 deg of rotation around the y axis, but vitually flat over the entire range from 0 to 88 deg.

14.  When a frontoparallel-oriented plane was placed in different positions within a cubical space filled with masking-dots, it was most easily detected at the center of the cube. Detectability diminished, therefore, where disparity was greatest in either the crossed or uncrossed direction.

In the third previously published monograph (Uttal, 1985), the following results emerged:

1.  Different three-dimensional stimulus types display only slight differences in detectability in the dotted-surface-in-dotted-mask type of task. A parabolic arch is detected slightly better than the average, and a double cubic and hyperbolic paraboloid are detected slightly less well than the average. However, these results are admittedly idiosyncratic and no general conclusions can be drawn from them. They seem to vary substantially with stimulus set, observers, and perhaps with the strategies used to "play the game" set by the experimenter. On the other hand, as will be elaborated shortly (see 3 below), different degrees of stretch of the same stimulus type showed vitually no effect on detectability despite the massive differences between the most extreme parabolic arch, for example, and all of the steps of lesser deformation down to a plane. These admittedly inconsistent results (from one experiment to another — a situation replicated, as we shall see, in the present work) suggest that some aspect of the stimulus set used within an experiment is important in determining the varying differential effects of stimulus shape. An explanation and understanding of the nature of these central aspects is yet to

be achieved. This was the first suggestion, however, that some cognitive influence might be penetrating what had been thought to be a predominately preattentive process.

2. Distributing the dots of the mask throughout the perceived space by means of disparity-controlled, dichoptic stereopsis did have the expected effect of functionally as well as perceptually dedensifying the mask and increasing performance when the stimulus-forms are generated from random-dot arrays.

3. The degree of deformation of *simple* types of polynominal-generated surfaces, however, has little effect on detectability when only one type of surface (i.e., a cylinder of various degrees of curvature) is used within an experiment. Simple types are defined as those in which the surfaces have only one maximum or minimum (e.g., a hemisphere). This null result obtains in spite of the fact that the *apparent* surface of a greatly distorted stimulus-form may have a greatly enlarged area compared to the plane from which it was generated and thus a substantially lower stimulus-form dot density. The contradiction between conclusions 2 and 3 constituted a major paradoxical outcome of the 1984 study. The implication of this conflict is that in this stereoscopic situation, the *apparent* signal-to-noise ratio is not a good predictor of performance. Variations in the apparent signal do not have the same effect as variations in the apparent noise. What does seem to work is the physical signal-to-noise ratio calculated from the retinal images as described subsequently in 6.

4. The degree of deformation from a plane to nonplanar stimulus surface, however, does exert a measurable and significant, though modest, influence on detectability when two or more maxima or minima are present on the nonplanar surface as exemplified by both the single and double dimensional cubics.

5. As the number of maxima and minima increases — for example, as regulated by the spatial frequency of a sinusoidal surface undulating in depth — detectability decreases further. However, close examination of such stimulus-forms indicates that the predominant portion of the decline in detectability due to variations in this parameter of form can actually be attributed to inadequate information being available to define the shape. At lower stimulus-form dot densities, the sampling density is insufficient for ever an ideal observer to reconstruct these complex forms. This outcome, therefore, can be attributed to a violation of the Nyquist limit — the sampling theorem. The human observer, however, does only slightly less well than the limits imposed by this sampling theorem — a remarkable outcome in itself.

6. The physical signal-to-noise ratio (i.e., as specified by the monocular stimulus) remains a strong determinant of the detectability of a form. Either increasing the actual stimulus-form dot density or decreasing the actual masking-dot density increases the detectability of the form. In sample experi-

ments in which the effect of three-dimensional form is negligible (and, thus, the effect of the apparent signal-to-noise ratio is minimal) over 90% of the variance in performance scores is accounted for by the physical signal-to-noise ratio alone. (However, it must not be forgotten that that story is different when one considers the *apparent* dot density.)

7. In general, even though the effects of form may be small or insignificant, performance scores do tend slightly to decrease as stimulus-forms deviate further from a plane.

8. In summary, there are some paradoxical or puzzling results in this third series of experiments that cannot be explained at the present time:

   a. Dedensifying the dots of a random-dot array stimulus-form by stretching it into three-dimensional space does not reduce the form's detectability. However, the stereoscopic procedure does strongly reduce the effect of a given number of masking-dots on random dot form detectability compared to monocular viewing. These two seemingly contradictory findings remain among the most distressing and inconsistent outcomes of this study.

   b. The size and mix of the stimulus set often influences the detectability of individual members of the set.

   c. The autocorrelation model, which had been so successful with two-dimensional stimuli, fails to predict the psychophysical results when three-dimensional stimuli are tested.

   d. Regular grid stimulus-forms display no sensitivity to nonplanar shape comparable to even that minor effect exhibited by forms generated from random-dot arrays.

   e. Obviously, there are multiple ways in which the various attributes of these dotted stimuli interact. Some of them remain obscure and are not yet well understood.

The results that have been obtained in the previous three studies and that are reported in abstract in this chapter are obviously incomplete and demand further investigation. That is the purpose of the present series of experiments.

# 3 The Experimental Paradigm

The purpose of this chapter is to introduce the reader to the methods and techniques that were used to collect the data in the psychophysical experiments reported here. As in any experimental situation, these methods are but the means to an end and it may be useful to reiterate in a somewhat paraphrased form what that end goal is. We are trying to answer a series of questions:

1. What is the effect of the geometry of the stimulus-form on its visibility (i.e., what is the effect of form on perception where "perception" is a catchall phrase collectively designating detection, discrimination, and recognition)? And as a corollary, how can we explain whatever form effects are obtained?

2. What is the effect of the signal-to-noise ratio on visibility? The informational properties dealt with in this case are approximated by the number of dots in the stimulus-form and the interfering visual noise respectively, however, other variables such as their "arrangement" make this a less than precise means of specifying the signal-to-noise attributes of the combined stimulus. It is important to remember, therefore, that the phrase "signal-to-noise ratio" may have multiple meanings. It may simply refer to the number of stimulus-form dots divided by the number of masking dots in the *physical* stimulus as just described. But it may also be used to refer to the *apparent* properties of the three-dimensional stimulus after processing by the stereopsis generating mechanism. The former need not be the same as the latter, and as we have seen, one (the physical signal-to-noise ratio) may predict the psychophysical outcome better than the other.

3. What is the effect of the task (detection, discrimination, or recognition) on the visual perception of three dimensional visual forms? In other words, is there a serial hierarchy of tasks or do they occur in parallel?

4. What effect does the type of sampling strategy used (random versus regular) have on the perception of these visual forms?

5. What is the effect on perception of the change in stimulus design from two dimensions to three dimensions?

These questions define the specific problems upon which we shall be working. But, from another point of view, they also define a space — a universe of discourse — encompassing the work I have pursued in the last decade. That universe was diagrammatically presented in Figure 1 and it is the definition of the rules that operate at each of the defined twelve conditions that is my immediate goal.

It is appropriate at this point to make a few general comments about the interrelationships among the elements of this universe — the stimulus-forms, the percepts, the equipment, the tasks, and the procedures. Our procedure defines an apparent stereoscopic space and certain apparent objects that have no correspondence in the physical reality of the stimulus world; the viewing volumes, the three-dimensional objects, and depth itself exist only in the perceived experience of the observer. In one of my earlier works (Uttal, 1985) in order to make this point emphatic, I noted that there is no possible physical realization of the three-dimensional space that is perceived by the observer at any of the several levels at which that space is represented prior to the merging of the neural signals representing the disparate retinal images somewhere in the brain. Indeed, despite the distinguished electrophysiological studies showing the anatomical loci of the fusions, we still have no idea of the point (or points) at which this neural information becomes the psychoneural equivalent of the experience in depth.

The point is that the perceived volume and its perceived contents — the stimulus-forms and the masks — in which the events with which we shall deal occur are abstractions in the digitally encoded storage of the computer, in the analog voltage representation subsequent to the digital and analog converters, on the dichoptic displays of the cathode ray tubes, and, perhaps also, (this is the key point) in the brain itself. Thus, a very major factor in defining the response of the observer should be the nature of the perceptual construction — the experience of depth. We are, to make this point very explicit, measuring attributes of visual perception that are probably less confounded by the physical attributes of the external world than is typical in this type of psychophysical study. The percepts with which we are dealing are constructions created by the visual system that are based upon computations of invariances and correspondences extracted from the pair of two-dimensional retinal images, but they are not explicit in the stimulus-forms presented to the two eyes; they are only implied and, as such, are much more creatures of our visual system than is usually the case. The results we obtain, therefore, speak very directly to the information processing properties of that visual system.

The next major point to be made is that both the stimuli and the means of degrading the stimuli we use — the addition of random dots to a nonrandom stimulus-form — are constant from one procedure to another. If not unique, this is certainly one of the rare instances in which *exactly* the same stimulus materials have been used to compare performance in several different tasks. In those experiments in which the same groups of observers have been used, a great deal of confidence can, therefore, be attributed to the relative values of the results we obtain. (As Appendix A indicates; not using the same observers can sometimes lead to a good deal of grief and embarrassment!)

The general procedure used in the experiments reported here is comparatively simple. A dotted stimulus-form or a pair of such forms, sampled either randomly or regularly, and embedded in a variable amount of random dots is presented to an observer. This establishes, at a minimum, a signal-to-noise extraction task, as well as providing a means of regulating the visibility of the stimulus-form, that is constant from one of the three visual tasks to another. The observer makes a simple psychophysical decision, in each case a multiple-alternative, forced-choice response, that indicates the detectability, the discriminability, or the recognizability of the particular stimulus-form or forms involved in that trial. What follows is simply flesh on this bare skeleton.

*Observers.*   A mix of male and female observers was utilized in this study on an hourly pay basis. When this study was being conducted at the University of Michigan, eight undergraduates, six of whom were males, were used. All eight of these University of Michigan observers served in all conditions of the three experiments (Numbers 1, 2, and 3) comparing the absolute levels of performance on the three different tasks — detection, discrimination, and recognition — that necessarily had to be carried out at separate times. The group of eight observers was separated into two subgroups of four each. Each subgroup was run in a different order of the three tasks to counterbalance any sequence effects. Though this precaution was taken, it probably was superfluous, as no long term learning effects extending beyond the first few hours of initial familiarization have ever been noticed in this kind of dot masking procedure. Our observers rarely improved their performance on the subsequent sequence of decreasing noise dot density following the initial sequence of increasing noise dot density.

The results presented in the following chapter indicate, furthermore, that there is no significant response bias either in the discrimination experiment or in the recognition experiment — the latter being the only case in which a response other than a simple button depression is requested. Once the general strategy is learned, therefore, the attributes of the stimulus and the set of which it is a part may be considered to be the main determinants of the observer's performance. This is not to say that the stimulus effects are simple or straightforward. Different sets of stimulus-forms seem to have a subtle influence on some of the outcomes of our experiments; the perception of a given stimulus is certainly influenced by the context in which it is presented to at least a certain extent.

When the later stages of the work were being carried out at the Naval Ocean Systems Center's Hawaii Lab, a group of female observers served in each of the remaining experiments. However, different groups of observers served in each of experiments 4 through 6. Experiment 7 used a separate group of 4 observers.

Each observer utilized in this study was pretested with anaglyph stereograms (Figure 8.1–2* from Julesz, 1971) and then with the haploscopic computer-driven displays to initially test stereoscopic competence. In addition, all accepted observers had normal or corrected-to-normal refractive vision. Each was then trained for approximately five hours in the experimental protocol before participating in any experiment.

*Apparatus.*    The study was carried out using a computer controlled system in which displays were generated, responses acquired, and the outcomes analyzed automatically. The stimulus displays utilized were random dot stereograms similar to the type originally suggested by Julesz (1960) that were degraded or masked by variable amounts of randomly placed dots, referred to as either visual "noise" or the dotted "mask."

The purpose of the degradation was to progressively stress the visual system by making the set of dotted forms less visible so that differences, if any, resulting from the task and/or the particular set of forms being tested could be measured. In the unmasked condition all of the dotted stimulus-forms were easily detected, discriminated, and recognized. When masked by additional randomly placed dots, however, differential effects of task and form became evident. Increasing masking dot density, thus, is a useful means of enhancing the *relative* effects of the various conditions and variables on performance even as the absolute levels of performance progressively fall; absolute number of masking dots, therefore, was one of the main independent variables used in all of the experiments reported here to selectively degrade the presented stimulus-forms.

Three-dimensional stimulus-forms were generated as dichoptic stereograms on the face of a Hewlett Packard 1311–B point plotting oscilloscope with a fast decay (P–24) phosphor. The manufacturer assures us in his technical manual that this signal trace was diminished in luminance down to .1 of 1% of its original value after a few microseconds. However, the tail end of

L                                    R

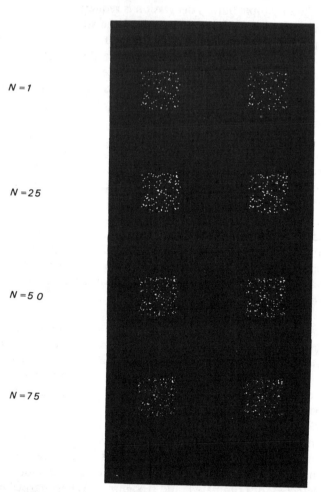

N = 1

N = 25

N = 5 0

N = 75

FIG. 3    Four sample stereoscopic stimuli showing a parabolic arch inserted in four different levels (N) of masking dots.

the diminishing trace may be quite long and because the dark adapted eye is exquisitely sensitive, we have no precise measure of the actual effective duration of the stimulus.

The observer viewed the screen from a distance of 71 cm. Each eye's image on the face of the screen subtended a visual angle of 5.4 × 5.4 deg. Rotary prisms were placed in front of each eye and individually adjusted by each observer to allow comfortable ocular convergence. The observer perceives an apparent volume that is as nearly cubical as can possibly be adjusted. The third (depth) dimension of the cube was defined by the disparity of the image:

The disparity was initially adjusted by the experimenter so that the volume enclosed was judged to be cubical. The disparity, thus arbitrarily defined, was subsequently determined to range from 14 min. of crossed disparity to 14 min. of uncrossed disparity with fixation (zero disparity) always placed at the center of the viewing cube. Figure 3 shows four examples of a stereoscopic stimulus in four different masking noise densities. If these stimuli are viewed in a stereoscope, they appear as parobolic arches, convex toward the observer. If they are viewed with crossed eyes, they appear to be concave towards the observer.

The images generated on the face of the oscilloscope were created from algorithms and stored prototypes within a Cromemco S–3 microcomputer. The digital representations of the three dimensional forms in the computer memory were converted by means of digital-to-analog converters into three voltage varying signals representing the $x$, $y$, and $z$ coordinates of a cartesian three-space. The voltages were then fed into a special purpose analog computer constructed from Optical Electronics, Inc. components (see Figure 4). The purpose of this analog computer was to convert the voltages representing the triplet set of numbers representing the three-dimensional coordinates of a dot into two pairs of numbers representing the two-dimensional coordinates of a disparate pair of dots — the left and right eye haploscopic images — that

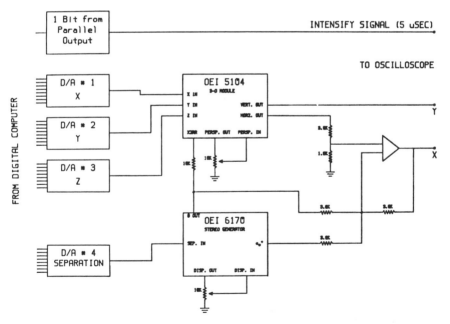

FIG. 4    The analog portion of the hybrid computer system used to display the stimulus stereograms in real time.

could stimulate the observer's perception of a three-dimensional shape in real time without burdening the computer with extensive and repetitive trigonometric calculations.

*Stimuli.*    The stimulus-forms used throughout this study consisted of seven nonplanar surfaces and one plane. The plane served as the prototype for the construction of five of the other seven forms — a circular cylinder, the parabolic arch, the $x$-cubic, the $x$-$y$ cubic, and the hyperbolic paraboloid. A decagon, approximating a circle, served as the prototype for the hemisphere and the paraboloid of rotation but was not itself used as a stimulus. Figure 5

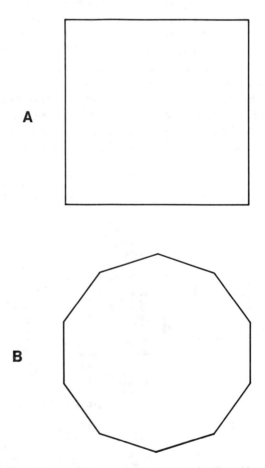

FIG. 5    The outline of the randomly sampled prototype stimuli used in some of the experiments. To keep stimulus density constant (rather than dot numerosity) the hemisphere and the paraboloid of rotation were constructed by decagonal prototypes rather than from the square prototype used for the other stimuli. See text for details.

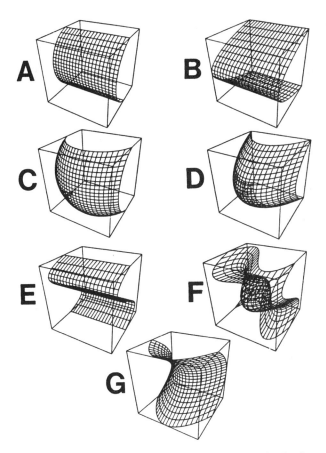

FIG. 6   Diagrammatic projective drawings of seven of the eight stimulus forms used in this study. (A planar surface was the eighth.) The actual stimuli did not have the grid lines nor the outline cube — the shape and volume attributes were suggested by the arrangement of the dots and had to be inferred by the observer's visual system.

presents the prototypes. In each case the prototype was deformed according to the rules of analytic geometry by applying a polynominal expression that "stretched" the prototype into one of the seven surfaces shown in Figure 6. The general polynominal expression is:

$$z = G (Ax^5 + Bx^4 + Cx^3 + Dx^2 + Ex + Ry^5 + Sy^4 + Ty^3 + Uy^2 + Vy + W)^F + H \qquad \text{(Eq. 6)}$$

By arbitrarily selecting the coefficients $(A,B,C,D,E,F,G,H,R,S,T,U,V,W)$ in this equation (including, of course, the option to set each to zero), it was possible to produce a wide variety of surfaces. Indeed, the expression could be easily generalized even further if components that were the products of $x$

and *y* and their powers were added to the general expression of Equation 6.

This polynomial expression was implemented within the context of a versatile, multipart stimulus generating program authored by John Brogan. Brogan's program first allowed the experimenter to create a prototypical planar surface (in this case either a square or a decagon) consisting of a constellation of randomly positioned dots or an experimenter-specified regular array of dots. The square and the decagon were about .8 deg smaller in angular subtense than the viewing cube, so that any subjective edges would be well within the region in which the masking dots occurred.

The second part of the program allowed the experimenter to deform this prototype into surfaces of the kinds exemplified in Figure 6. These random surfaces, as well as those shown in Figure 7, are, however, only diagrammatically represented. In actual fact, the observer saw neither the grid-like sur-

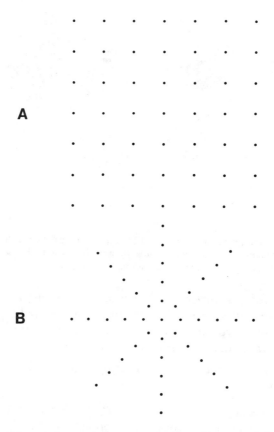

FIG. 7   Typical regularly sampled protype stimuli used in some of the experiments. Again, to keep the dots relatively constant in density and to achieve symmetry, the number of dots had to be adjusted slightly. See text for details.

TABLE 2

The generating equations for the seven nonplanar stimulus-forms used in this study. The eighth form — the plane — was characterized by the equation $Z = 2048$. The numbers used in this equation are not important. They are selected mainly to calibrate the particular digital to analog converters and the oscilloscope used in our system so that forms of the proper shape and position will be presented to the observer. Other display systems could produce the same stimuli even when different coefficients and exponents are used in the mathematical analyses.

| Stimulus Form | Generating Equation | Coefficients |
|---|---|---|
| Cylinder | $z = G(-y^2 + W)^{1/2} + H$ | $W = 948676$ <br> $H = 2535$ <br> $G = -1$ |
| Parabolic Arch | $z = Gy^2 + H$ | $G = .002$ <br> $H = 1099$ |
| Hemisphere | $z = G(-x^2 - y^2 + W)^{1/2} + H$ | $W = 948676$ <br> $H = 2535$ <br> $G = -1$ |
| Paraboloid of Rotation | $z = G(x^2 + y^2) + H$ | $G = .002$ <br> $H = 1085$ |
| Cubic in one dimension | $z = G(.001y^3 - 948.67y) + H$ | $G = .0025$ <br> $H = 2048$ |
| Cubic in two dimensions | $z = G(.001x^3 - 948.6x + .001y^3 - 948.6y) + H$ | $G = .001$ <br> $H = 2048$ |
| Hyperbolic Paraboloid | $z = G(x^2 - y^2) + H$ | $G = -.001$ <br> $H = 2048$ |

face nor the outlines of the cube. These extra lines are presented here only to help readers of this monograph to visualize these forms. In the experimental presentation, the cube was defined only by the extent of the masking-dots and the nonplanar stimulus surface. The polynominal expressions for the seven nonplanar forms are presented in Table 2.

It must be emphasized that the stimuli were all dotted forms similar to those shown in Figure 3 and the dots making up the surfaces were distributed either at random or in regular order. The geometrical shapes to which we refer are simply the mathematical surfaces to which the sampling dots are constrained. It is solely the distribution of noise and stimulus dots that defines the viewing space and the stimulus-forms respectively. The geometrical surfaces used as stimuli were all aligned in a fronto-parallel plane with the main axis of convexity apparently protruding towards the observer by appropriate selection of the disparities.

In some experiments, the stimulus forms varied in the density of the array of dots from which they were formed. In others, only a single density — an intermediate value — was used for each of the stimulus-forms. In those former cases in which stimulus-dot density varied, the eight stimulus-forms were presented at three different dot densities — thus providing 24 distinct stimuli. Six of the stimulus forms — the plane, the arch, the cylinder, the one-dimensional cubic, the two-dimensional cubic, and the saddle — those generated from the square prototype plane — contained either 64, 49, or 36 dots depending on the required stimulus dot density. The hemisphere and paraboloid of rotation were generated from decagonal prototypes that subtended 79% ($\pi/4$) of the surface area of the square prototype. Therefore, in order to keep the density of the randomly arrayed dots in the these slightly smaller, nearly circular, surface areas constant (an arbitrary decision — dot numerosity could have been kept constant instead) the three prototypes in this case contained 50, 38, and 28 dots respectively, depending upon the desired dot density.

The count was necessarily slightly different for the lower density, regular, grid-like stimuli used in some of the experiments in which the visibility of regular and random arrays were compared. To maintain symmetry in the single intermediate dot density used in that case, we utilized a square array of 49 dots for the plane, cylinder, arch, one-dimensional cubic, two-dimensional cubic and the saddle. However, 41 dots had to be used in defining the nearly circular prototypes from which the hemisphere and the paraboloid of rotation were constructed in order to keep that regular stimulus symmetrical. Figure 7 shows the two prototypes used in that case.

The mask in all cases consisted of an array of dots that was randomly distributed in the 5.4 × 5.4 deg × 28 min of disparity cubical viewing space and that varied in numerosity according to the needs of each experiment. Stimulus-forms were created on the display by repetitively plotting a series of dots at a sufficiently high speed so that the display appeared to be constantly present without apparent flicker throughout the entire one sec period that each presentation lasted. The dots defining the stimulus-form were constrained to lie on the surface specified by the particular coefficients of Equation 6 that were utilized; as noted, the dots of the masking visual noise were always distributed throughout the entire stereoscopically defined viewing volume.

*Psychophysical Procedure.*    Responses were acquired in two ways. For the detection and discrimination experiments, only two alternative responses were allowed. The observer asserted *in which of two sequential presentations a form had been present* in the detection experiment, or *whether the two presentations were the same or different* in the discrimination experiment, by depressing one of two hand-held push buttons. The left button indicated either "first" or "the same" in the two experiments respectively. The recognition experiment presented only a single stimulus, however, it required more alternative responses since the observer's response was the actual naming of the eight stimulus forms. This requirement was satisfied by using an Interstate Electronics Corporation VR200 voice recognition terminal. This device was trained to respond to each speaker's voice in a preliminary procedure lasting approximately three minutes at the beginning of each experimental session. Because of the moderate level of recognition accuracy provided by the VR200, it was necessary to also have the computer respond through a VOTRAX voice generation device what utterance it had acquired. The observer then accepted or rejected the computer's decision by depressing one of the two hand-held push-buttons.

In each of the three types of experiment—detection, discrimination, and recognition—the sequence of a trial began with a one sec dichoptic pair of fixation dots used by the observer to define the zero disparity center of the viewing cube and to help in establishing steady fixation, dot-pair correspondances, and good stereoscopic fusion. This was done to reduce the demand on the observer's ability to achieve good stereopsis as much as possible. Such a strategy also had the very important effect of removing our research from the domain of "How do observers solve the correspondance problem?" and placing it in the domain of "How do observers process stereoscopic images once they have been constructed?" This is the domain of choice for this study and it must be distinguished from the work of those interested in the mechanisms and processes underlying the initial construction of the stereoscopic experience.

In the two types of two-presentation experiments (detection and discrimination), the one sec exposure of the pair of fixation points was followed by the first of the two stimulus presentations. A second pair of fixation points, also lasting for one second, was then presented followed by the second stimulus presentation. The computer then waited for the appropriate button depression and then reinforced the observer by presenting either a plus or minus sign indicating a correct response or an error.

The remaining type of experiment (recognition) was characterized by the fact that only a single stimulus presentation occurred. The one sec pair of fixation dots was followed by a single stimulus and then by a question mark. This signal helped the observer to synchronize his utterance with the acoustic "open window" during which the voice recognition system could accept the verbal response. Figure 8 shows the design of the types of trials characterizing the three different tasks.

Data was analyzed by a system of special-purpose statistical programs. Detection experiments were initially accumulated into the raw proportion correct for each observer upon completion of each session and then subsequently analyzed as described below. The discrimination and recognition experiments were, in addition, initially analyzed by a system of programs that computed error matrices for all combinations of the eight stimuli. The discrimination "error" matrix tabulated the number of times that either two

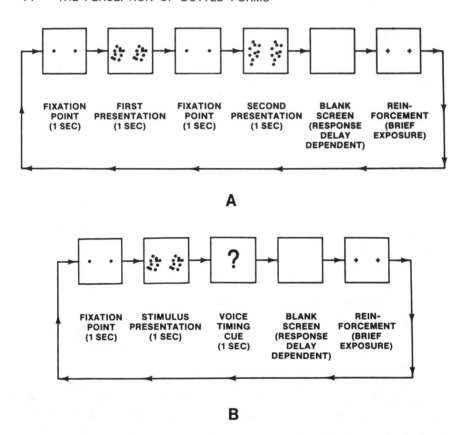

FIG. 8. (a) The sequence of events in a single trial in the detection and discrimination experiments. (b) The sequence of events in a single trial in the recognition experiments.

identical stimulus-forms were reported to be different or two different stimuli were reported to be the same. In the case of the recognition experiment, only a single "error" matrix was tabulated indicating the erroneous responses given to the 24 stimuli. The data from all three types of experiments was subsequently pooled across observers or pooled according to various experimental design requirements by means of other statistical programs.

# 4 Experimental Design and Results

In this chapter, I present the rationale and design of the series of experiments that have been carried out to explore form perception in the universe of dotted stimulus-forms within which this study was conducted. The particular experiments were virtually predefined by the diagram shown in Figure 1. To briefly review, however, one major goal was to explore the effect of the perceptual task, sampling strategy, and geometrical form on the visibility of a set of geometrical forms produced by distorting a prototypical plane by means of a general purpose polynomial generating expression (See Eq. 6). The application of this expression to produce a family of generating equations produced the seven forms shown in Figure 6. These seven, along with the prototypical plane, were the only stimulus-forms used throughout this study. Though the dot density of both the stimulus and the mask could vary independently and the dots could be either regularly or randomly organized, each is the most extremely distorted version of that particular geometrical surface that could be contained in our viewing space.

In order to achieve the dual goals of determining the effects of form and task and to make the comparison as precise as possible, it is necessary to reduce one particular source of variance—the individual differences that previously confounded all experiments of this type—to a minimum. That was accomplished by the logistically difficult task of keeping the same group of observers throughout the entire time period that Experiments 1, 2, and 3 were being carried out, on the one hand, and for both parts of Experiment 4, 5, and 6 respectively, on the other. Experiment 7 used an entirely different group of observers. Thus, five different groups of observers were used. Under most previous conditions holding a single group for more than a single experiment had proven to be nearly impossible, but a system of bonuses, alternate observers, and gentle cajolery did succeed for the first three experiments.

Experiments 1, 2 and 3, therefore, used the same stimuli, the same observers, and nearly identical psychophysical procedures to determine both the impact of the task – detection, discrimination, and recognition – and the influence of form on performance. As usual, we also acquired a relatively large amount of data because of our automatic experimental control procedures and this also added to the precision of the comparisons.

The second major theme that characterizes the series of experiments reported here concerns the impact of the kind of sampling used to define each of the stimuli. Although the exploration of the effects of the task on performance (Experiments 1, 2, and 3) was carried out using stimuli that were all sampled by a random procedure, Experiment 4, 5, and 6 introduced an additional condition – some of the stimulus-forms were constructed from a prototype that itself was a regular, circularly symmetrical grid or rectangular lattice of dots. With the exception of the hemisphere and the paraboloid of rotation, which was extruded from a prototype shaped like a planar decagon, the regular prototype was a square grid of 49 dots. The two exceptional cases – the hemisphere and the paraboloid of rotation – were constructed by distorting a decagonally, but regularly, organized array of dots as has been shown earlier in Figure 7. As I have noted earlier, since the surface area of the square grid was $4/\pi$ times as large as the decagon and because it was arbitrarily decided to keep the dot density, rather than the number of dots, nearly constant, 41 symmetrically arranged dots were used in the two surfaces generated from the decagonal prototypes. This is slightly different than the number (38) used in the randomly organized decagonal comparison stimulus, but as we shall see, the results of this comparison are strong enough to assure that the difference between the two sets of stimuli cannot be accounted for by the small difference in stimulus-dot numerosity.

Using these regularly organized stimulus-forms we were able to extend our examination of the effects of signal-to-noise ratio, task, and form from the random stimuli (with which Experiments 1, 2, and 3 dealt) to the comparative effects of regular and random stimuli. Experiments 5 and 6 extend the comparison between response scores to random and regularly organized stimuli made earlier for detection (Uttal, 1984) to the other two tasks – discrimination and recognition – respectively. Experiment 4 is a near replication of the earlier work. However, it uses a slightly different grid of stimuli – a circularly symmetric array for the paraboloid and the hemisphere – rather than a rectangularly arranged grid of dots that was used in the original 1984 study. Furthermore, Experiments 4, 5, and 6 all used the set of seven forms shown in Figure 6 and a plane rather than a single form of various degrees of deformation.

As we shall subsequently see, there were substantial surprises awaiting as this series of comparative experiments unfolded; surprises that further diminished our confidence that universal rules of dotted form perception exist that can be generalized across conditions. Rather, the main outcome of this series of experiments supports the idea that a set of relatively independent rules or processes exist in the visual nervous system, even within the narrow confines of this dotted-form-in-dotted-mask paradigm.

A caveat must be expressed here (and is repeated later) concerning Experiments 4, 5, and 6. In all three of these experiments, the use of the regularly sampled stimuli introduces a monocular artifact confounding the straightforward interpretation of the obtained results. In addition to the disparity cues, the observer has the linear periodicity cue with which to work when dealing with those regular stimulus-forms. As we shall see, this influences our interpretation of these experiments in a significant way.

Finally, we include in the discussion of Experiment 7 an abbreviated version of the rationale, design, and results of a very important control study carried out by Wilfred Kincaid of the University of Michigan and myself in which it is shown that no local regions of spuriously large stimulus dot density could account for the fact that the three-dimensional shape of a form did not influence it's detectability.

## DESIGN AND RATIONALE

### Experiment 1

Experiments 1, 2, and 3 examined the effects of detection, discrimination, and recognition respectively on dotted form perception using the same observers, the same stimuli, and nearly the same procedure. The main goal was, thus, to determine the effect of the specific visual task on dotted-form perception. It is, therefore, also a test of a hierarchical model of visual information processing as described in Chapter 1.

The first of these three experiments replicated the design of one of our earlier detection studies (Uttal, 1984). The motivation for this replication was both the need to collect comparable data from the same group of observers utilized in Experiments 2 and 3 and to act as a link back to the earlier work. As indicated earlier, the observer's task in this case was to report in which of two sequential one sec presentations a dotted stimulus-form had been presented by depressing one of two hand-held push-buttons. One of these two stimuli contained the stimulus-form and a number of randomly positioned masking dots. The other contained the same masking dots plus a number of additional randomly positioned "dummy dots" equal to the number of dots in the stimulus form. After each response a plus or a minus sign was displayed on the oscilloscope to indicate if the observer's choice had been correct or incorrect. The next trial was then automatically initiated.

Experiment 1 was carried out on seven successive days during which the masking dot densities were progressively increased from zero to 300 dots in 50–dot increments. The 24 stimuli (the eight forms presented at three different sampling densities as described on page 42) were presented in random order during each daily session. Twenty four randomly sampled (irregular) stimuli were used in this experiment. Eight were high density (64 and 50 dots), eight were medium density (49 and 38 dots), and eight were low density (36 and 28 dots) with the lower number in each pair indicating the numerosity of the dots in the paraboloid and hemisphere (whose area was $\pi/4$ times the area of the other forms) and the higher number indicating the numerosity of the dots in the other six stimuli. Approximately 600 trials occurred in each one hour long session.

## Experiment 2

The second experiment was carried out using the same group of observers who participated in Experiment 1, but in this case they were asked to discriminate (rather than detect) between pairs of stimulus-forms selected from the same set of 24 stimulus-forms used in Experiment 1. The observers were successively presented with two of the geometrical forms and asked to specify if they were the same or different: Both presentations contained organized stimulus-forms. The pairs chosen to be discriminated in each trial were constrained so that only equal dot densities were compared with each other. This was done to assure that the task depended upon shape alone and not upon a not-so-subtle density cue. As in the detection experiment, the required response was a two-alternative button press. In this case, however, the button depressed indicated whether the two presentations contained stimuli that appeared to the observer to be the same or to be different. The random noise dots were also constrained to be identical in each of the two presentations by appropriate programming manipulations. As in the detection experiment, the observer was immediately reinforced with a plus or a minus sign to indicate the correctness or incorrectness of the decision.

The discrimination experiment involved one other parameter — it was possible to specify in what proportion of the trials the two stimuli should be identical. For this experiment, it was decided to use 33% as the value of this factor. That is, the two stimuli were constrained to be identical on a randomly chosen one-third of the trials. This is an important variable because it does interact with the number of alternatives to determine the level at which the observer would perform if he or she saw nothing and was merely guessing.

All of the stimuli used in this experiment were constructed from the same randomly sampled prototypes that were used in Experiment 1, thus continuing the commitment to control the dot density rather than the area of the stimuli by adjusting the number of dots to the area of the prototype plane.

The discrimination experiment was carried out on 14 consecutive days. On seven of these days, the masking dot density was sequentially increased in steps of 50 from 0 to 300 dots. On the last seven days the order was reversed and the masking dot density was progressively decreased from 300 to 0 dots. As in all of our experiments, the scores for each observer were very close on the equivalent masking dot densities obtained during the rising and falling portions of this sequence of daily sessions. This indicates that little if any cognitive or strategic learning was taking place after initial training. This is consistent with the current consensus and my own conviction that this form of visual information processing mainly occurs at a relatively lower level than "cognitive" processing; it is predominantly preattentive and precognitive, and thus not subject to the usual experiential influences once the observer is trained in the basics of the procedure. As we shall see later in our analysis of the results, response bias also appears to be minimal and the observer's decisions seem to be mainly driven by the stimuli.

## Experiment 3

Experiment 3 required the observer to name which one of the eight geometrical forms had been presented by orally uttering a code name ("cylinder," "arch," "hemisphere," "paraboloid," "cubic," "double," "saddle," and "surface") into a microphone mounted just below the convergence prisms at mouth level. These code words wre used to signify the (1) circular cylinder, (2) the parabolic arch, (3) the hemisphere, (4) the paraboloid of rotation, (5) the $y$- or one-dimensional cubic, (6) the $x$-$y$ or two-dimensional cubic, (7) the hyperbolic paraboloid, and (8) the square planar surface. These words were chosen to both maximize the ease of learning for the observers and the discriminability of the sounds to the speech recognition system.

The utterance was acquired by the speech recognition system, coded into one of the eight names previously assigned to a vocabulary file, and echoed through the speech output system. If the computer's utterance agreed with the observer's, the observer depressed the left one of the two hand held push buttons thus accepting the input as a valid datum. If the computer's utterance disagreed with his utterance (indicating a misidentification by the speech recognition system), the observer pushed the other button, the computer replied "try again" through it's voice output, and the observer repeated the response. For most well trained observers the rejection rate (i.e., the number of "try agains") was only a few percent of the total number of utterances during the course of the experiment. Again, the observer was immediately reinforced with a plus or minus sign when both the computer and the observer agreed that the appropriate response had been acquired.

The recognition experiment was also carried out over fourteen days using the same stimuli as were used in Experiments 1 and 2. However, pilot studies with randomly sampled stimuli had shown that the performance level fell much faster than in the detection and discrimination experiments.[6] At a noise dot density of 150, performance had deteriorated to a level at which we have previously found our observers to become restive and demoralized and the experiment was, therefore, truncated at that point. After progressively increasing the noise in 25 dot increments for seven days, it was progressively reduced over the same range and with the same step size. In the recognition experiment, 350 trials were typically collected in each one hour session.

## Experiment 4

Before I discuss the rationale, procedures, and results of Experiments 4, 5, and 6, I must reiterate that parts of these three experiments are confounded by a monocular cue. The regular stimuli in Experiments 4, 5, and 6 contain straight lines in each eye's image (as shown in Figure 7) that can help the observer distinguish one stimulus from another. This monocular cue is such that the regular stimuli have an advantage that makes the results of a comparison between stereoscopic regularly and randomly sampled stimulus-forms equivocal. The results reported here are presented in that spirit — that they are confounded. If the results had turned out as they had previously (the reader is again referred to Appendix A) — an advantage to the randomly sampled stimuli — this confounding could have been overlooked and the results would have been *very* interesting. As we shall see in this section and in Appendix A, however, this was not the case and the results we have obtained are much less exciting. Nevertheless, let's consider the situation in more detail.

Each of the Experiments 4, 5, and 6 reported in the following sections consist of two parts. The first is an assay of the observer's performance when presented with the eight stimulus-forms sampled by a random algorithm. That is, the position of any dot on any of these surfaces is random on the projected $x$-$y$ plane. The second part is an assay of their performance when presented with the same forms, but sampled such that the points fall on a regular two-dimensional grid on the projection of these forms onto the $x$-$y$ plane.

These three two-part experiments were motivated by two of our earlier results. One was the very surprising and counterintuitive, yet strong, result that

---

[6]As we shall see, however, this turned out not to be true when regular stimuli were used in Experiment 6. These stimuli remained reasonably recognizable even at noise dot densities of 300.

random three-dimensional stimulus-forms were *detected* much more easily than the same nonplanar surfaces constructed from regular prototypes. The unexpectedness of this result was substantial, but this unexpected outcome was accepted and my willingness to do so was reinforced when a review of the literature demonstrated that this surprising result is exactly predicted by statistical sampling theory. Agricultural and social scientist practioners of the sampling statistics had long argued that random samples are superior to regular samples when the surfaces to be reconstructed are varying in a smooth and uniform fashion. The human observer, in other words, seemed to have evolved in such a way that he performed precisely as a remote and esoteric mathematical theorem predicted that he should. Another way to make this point is that the quality of the neural information processing algorithm that was theoretically optimal seemed not to be lost in the midst of the other needs of the visual system. As we shall see, a conceptual trap was being set into which I all too willingly fell.

It must also not be forgotten that the comparable results in two dimensions indicated, quite to the contrary, that regularity was the prepotent stimulus property even though the opposite seemed to be true in three dimensions. Indeed, this was the basis of the second motivating argument for this fourth experiment; the results being obtained in this series of experiments seemed not to generalize from one experiment to the next. We were beginning to become a little more conservative and unwilling to make what would have seemed to be the simplest and most obvious logical leaps from one condition to even a very closely related one without an empirical test.

Experiment 4, therefore, was a partial replication of several earlier experiments (supplementary Experiments 14, 15, 16, and 17 in Uttal, 1985) but, unavoidably, it did use a completely different set of observers. It was carried out in order to deny or substantiate the putative, but as we shall see now discredited, Rule of Random Sampling — the assertion that random sampling provides a better level of detection than does regular sampling. It was deemed necesary to do so because Experiments 5 and 6, which were carried out before Experiment 4 chronologically, if not logically, had produced results that were opposite to our previous rule — regular stimuli were discriminated and recognized better than random ones in those two experiments by the observers used in our new locale. The replication was also necessary because two of the regular stimuli (the hemisphere and the paraboloid of rotation) in this new experiment were constructed from circularly symmetrical prototypes rather than from rectangular grids as had been used in the earlier experiments. Both the regular and irregular stimuli were the medium density (49 and 41 dots) ones shown in Figure 5 and Figure 7. This single medium density represents only a single one of the five densities (81, 64, 49, 36, 25) used in the original 1984 work in which random sampling had appeared to be superior than regular sampling in the detection task. Another major difference between this experiment and the ones in the earlier study (Uttal, 1984) was that the stimulus set here consisted of the most extreme versions of eight different forms rather than the set of progressively more distorted versions of a single polynomial generated shape. As was now becoming routine, a major surprise awaited us when the results were analyzed.

The standard detection paradigm was used with the outcome of a two-alternative, forced choice decision indicated by which of two push buttons was depressed. The eight stimuli were presented in random order on fourteen successive days with masking dot densities varying from 0 to 300 dots in 50-dot steps, first in ascending order and then in descending order. Data was subsequently pooled for each pair of equivalent masking dot densities.

The experiment was then rerun with the same medium dot density, but randomly sampled, stimuli in the same sequence of masking dot densities to provide as exact as possible comparison with the same group of observers. Because of a scheduling problem we were able to run only one sequence of increasing masking dot densities in this experiment, unlike the others in which both increasing and decreasing masking dot densities were carried out. Though the resulting data are somewhat noiser than would have been obtained if both an ascending and descending sequence had been run, the negligible differences in absolute levels of performance in the two series makes it an acceptable procedure.

It is important once again to reiterate as I conclude this discussion that the detection, discrimination, and recognition of regular stimuli, like those used in the present study, are subject to a unavoidable confounding. That limit on the value of these experiments is based upon the fact that there is, with all regularly sampled stimuli, a monocular cue present — retinotopic straight dotted lines. The problem is that this monocular cue might produce spuriously high performance scores that might exceed those obained with three-dimensional stimuli that were purely disparity driven and thus depended solely upon dichoptic cues. I hope my readers forgive this redundancy but the point is central to any consideration of the findings of Experiment 4, 5, and 6 and it *must not* be overlooked in a hasty reading of the details of these experiments.

## Experiment 5

The fifth experiment in this study is designed to compare the discrimination performance of a new set of observers (neither the carefully maintained set that had been used throughout the first three experiments nor the ones used in Experiment 4) on regularly and randomly sampled, medium density, three dimensional surfaces. For the regular stimulus forms, six were constructed from a square prototype consisting of 49 linearly arrayed dots and two were constructed from a circularly symmetrical array consisting of 41 dots as shown in Figure 7.

The design of this fifth experiment — a comparison of the discriminability of regular and randomly sampled surfaces — required only that the intermediate densities of the randomly sampled stimuli be used in this experiment. However, because of an earlier computer failure some of the error and correct matrix data that should have been acquired in Experiment 2 had been lost. The repetition of the random stimulus discrimination experiment that had to be carried out to recover these data was, therefore, slightly more complicated than required if it had been carried out specifically for the purposes of this experiment. Thus, in this replication all three of the random dot densities (the high density — 65 and 51; the medium density — 49 and 38; and the low density — 36 and 28 dots respectively) of the eight stimulus forms were presented. Therefore, there were 24 different randomly sampled stimuli from which a single form could be randomly selected for each trial. This does make the number of alternatives in each discrimination task greater, but our experience with this kind of stimulus material suggested that a fair comparison could still be made with the eight regular stimuli of the other part of the experiment. It is, therefore, only the comparison between the medium density subset of the extended set of randomly sampled forms and the regularly sampled set of eight forms that is reported in the results section of this chapter. The tabulation of the error matrices for this experiment are presented in the consideration of the results of Experiment 2.

After the standard four days of preliminary familiarization and training, the observers were sequenced through a series of seven daily sessions in which the random visual masking dot density was progressively increased from 0 to 300 dots in 50–dot increments. These masking dots were superimposed upon the eight regularly sampled, medium density stimulus-forms. The noise dot density was then progressively reduced over seven days to give an equivalent descending sequence. the experiment was then repeated using the 24 high, medium, and low density, randomly sampled stimulus-forms.

## Experiment 6

The sixth experiment in this report is a comparison of the recognizability of the eight regular and the eight random, medium density, stimulus-forms. The motivation is the same in this case as in the fourth and fifth experiments — it is no longer possible to have confidence in simple extrapolations of the results from one of the twelve conditions shown in Figure 1 to another. Each must be individually tested to determine what the rules of visual perception are that obtain in that particular situation. In this case, we used the recognition mode described earlier. Two stimulus sets were used, one consisting of the eight stimulus-forms randomly sampled at the intermediate dot density (49 and 38 dots respectively) and the other consisting of the same eight stimulus-forms but sampled by the regular matrices shown in Figure 7 and containing 49 or 41 dots respectively.

A pilot study showed that the recognizability of the regular stimulus-forms was substantially greater than that of the random forms. Therefore, the sequence of experimental sessions for the regularly sampled stimuli consisted of seven successive days in which the masking dots density was increased progressively from 0 to 300 dots in 50–dot increments. The sequence was then repeated in descending order and the two sequences pooled to produce the results of the experiment. The randomly sampled stimuli were tested in fourteen sessions with noise-dot-densities first increasing in 25–dot increments from 0 to 150 dots and then decreasing in the opposite sequence.

## Experiment 7

Wilfred Kincaid, of the University of Michigan, and I have carried out an experiment that we believe is a very important control that responds to one recurring misinterpretation of the dot-masking work. This criticism, which we believe to be unjustified, suggests that an artifact exists in our work that accounts for the lack of a stable influence of the form of a dotted stimulus on detection, discrimination, and recognition. Throughout this entire series of experiments, we have generally found that perception is only very weakly or very idiosyncratically influenced by the three-dimensional shape of the stimulus. This conclusion was based, however, on studies of planes and of curved stimuli of the kind generated here from the polynomial expression (Eq. 6) with which we have already become familiar. As we have seen, the planes are fronto-parallel, centrally placed, and of nearly the same 5.4 deg height and width as the viewing cube. The curved surfaces are portions of cylinders, hemispheres, parabolic arches, and other forms generated by applying this standard polynomial generating rule to a prototype plane.

As reported in Uttal (1984) the probability of correct responses (for fixed numbers of stimulus and masking dots) decreased only slightly with increasing departure from the prototype plane for each class of surface. In fact, many of the most extremely distorted nonplanar surfaces showed no measurable differences in detection scores from the planar stimulus. It was only when the surface had more than one maximum or minimum (in depth) that barely significant effects were obtained. This result, revealing a substantial insensitivity to the third-dimensional aspects of these stereoscopic forms, suggests that a limit exists on the perceiver's ability to process this kind of information.

One a priori reason for having expected effects of three-dimensional form is that the perceived surface areas of the apparently three-dimensional curved surfaces are greater than the apparent area of the plane. Given that the same number of dots was used in each case, the *apparent density* should be effectively less for the curved surfaces than for the plane. Thus, it seemed that detectability should have decreased even if the density of the masking dots remained constant. The experimental results thus suggest that the stereoscopically constructed third- (depth) dimension, which has to be indirectly calculated from invariances in the disparity information, is not processed in the same way in this context as the other two planar dimensions, which are physically projected onto the retina. An often suggested counterargument to this line of reasoning is that the observer might be selectively directing most of his attention to restricted subportions of the curved surface that are nearly fronto-parallel, where the densities remain locally constant.

The issue of local region cues is important enough that Kincaid and I judged it desirable to seek further experimental evidence concerning the effect of apparent, as opposed to real, density on detectability. To this end, we noted that comparing a fronto-parallel plane with a tilted plane (instead of with a curved surface) would avoid the local region complication as well as other potential artifacts that might be associated with curvature as such because all regions of a tilted plane would have the same slope.

In an earlier study, Uttal, Fitzgerald, and Eskin (1975) such a comparison had, in fact, been made. However, in that experiment the frontal projection area of the plane was controlled so that it varied with the angle of rotation; thus the density of the dots of the stimulus-form was constant on the apparent plane regardless of its orientation as it varied in its frontal projection. This difference makes it impossible to settle the issue raised here with these data. Accordingly, Kincaid and I carried out the experiment described below. The main difference is that a regular parallelepiped (rather than a cubical volume) was used as the viewing space and the sides of the rectangular plane were anchored to the sides of the space rather than restricted to the projected dimensions of a rotated version of the original fronto-parallel plane.

In this experiment, the dots of the stimulus-form in each presentation lay in a single vertical plane with its axis of rotation passing through the center of the rectangular stimulus volume as shown in Figure 9. In any trial, the plane could be oriented to any one of 10 possible positions, ranging from fronto-parallel to diagonal. In the fronto-parallel orientation, the plane extended across the width of the rectangular viewing space. In the diagonal position, however, the plane extended from the left front edge to the right rear edge of the viewing space. In all cases, the plane extended completely across the rectangular viewing space; that is, its top and bottom edges lay on the top and bottom surfaces of the stimulus region and its left and right edges were anchored to the left and right sides of the stimulus region — the sides along which the vertical edges of the plane side as the plane is rotated. Thus the dots lay in a rectangle whose height was 3 deg and whose width varied from 3 deg to $(3^2 + 5.4^2)$ deg or 6.18 deg. Hence the maximally rotated diagonal plane had 2.06 times the apparent area of the fronto-parallel one. Of course, the retinal projections of the left and right eye images remained nearly constant.

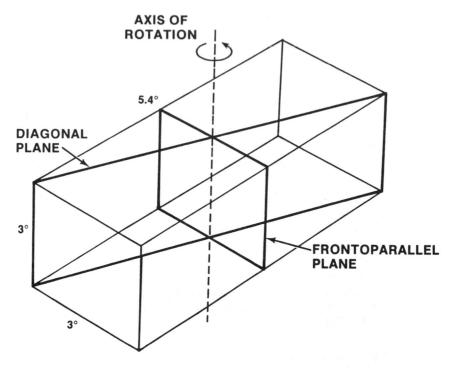

FIG. 9    The arrangement of the stimuli in Experiment 7 showing the effect on apparent surface area as the plane is rotated around the *y* axis in the rectangular volume.

The experiment was carried out in fourteen successive, daily sessions. During the first seven days the masking dot density was progressively increased from 25 to 200 dots in the following order: 25, 50, 100, 125, 150, 175, and 200. During the second seven days the masking dot density was decreased in reversed order.

Thirty distinctly different planar stimuli were used in this study; ten with 25, ten with 36, and ten with 49 randomly positioned dots. Ten different orientations were used, varying from a fronto-parallel plane to an orientation of 64.1 deg (the maximum diagonal from the front corner of the rectangular space to the rear corner) in equal angular steps of 7.12 deg.

## RESULTS

### Experiments 1, 2, and 3

The results of the Experiments 1, 2, and 3 are shown in a heavily pooled form in Figures 10 and 11, respectively, as function of the masking dot density. Figure 10 shows the data from the three experiments pooled across all observers, all geometrical forms, and all stimulus-form dot densities. This figure presents one of the major results of this study — the comparison of performance under the three different task conditions. The three parametric curves appear to be distinctly different at first glance. In particular: (1) the recognition data appears to drop off much more rapidly than do the other two curves; (2) the detection and discrimination data actually cross over; and (3) all three curves asymptote to different levels.

To more accurately depict the relationship of these three curves, however, other considerations must be incorporated into the analysis. First, the levels of chance performance in the three experiments are not all equal. In the recognition experiment there are eight alternative responses; in the detection experiment there are two; and in the discrimination experiment the situation is even more complicated — the proportion of trials in which the two stimuli are the same is .33. Therefore, with the two possible alternative responses (same and different) the level of indiscriminate performance could initially be either 33% or 66% (depending on which key was depressed), but as the observer acquires information about the actual distribution of same and different presentations, the indiscriminate scores could vary as his subjective response probabilities are adjusted.

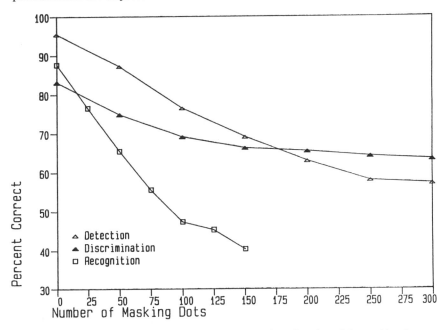

FIG. 10    The results of Experiments 1, 2, and 3 plotted as a function of the masking dot density and pooled across all other independent variables and plotted with task as the parameter.

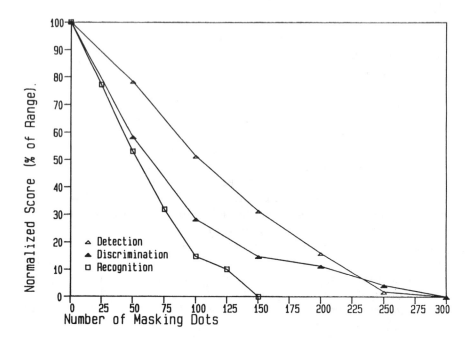

FIG. 11    The data from Experiments 1, 2, and 3 that were displayed in Figure 10 in a raw form, but normalized to more appropriately show the relative effects of the task on performance.

To more correctly compare these three curves, therefore, the data shown in Figure 10 have been replotted in Figure 11 in a normalized form. The raw scores have had the minimum pooled score subtracted and then have been divided by the difference between the maximum and minimum pooled scores to bring all three functions to the same scale. The transformed scores from the three tasks display much greater similarity than had been evident in the raw data. There remains, and this is the key point, a residual ordering of performance as a function of the task even when normalized. The effect of masking dot density is still clearly differential; performance drops off more rapidly for recognition, discrimination, and detection in that order.

The curious discrepancy appearing in the raw data—i.e., that performance in the discrimination task is superior in some instances to performance in the detection task, although reduced, is not eliminated and cannot be ignored. Yet, as we have already seen, this a priori absurd result is actually plausible in some circumstances. This logical plausibility and the robustness of the data presented here suggests that, in fact, our observers may be pooling information across the two presentations to discriminate forms at what appear to be lower levels than those at which the forms can be detected. However, an alternative explanation may be that they are pooling information over the entire gamut of experimental trials to alter their response probabilities and thus to bias their scores above that determined solely by the perceptual influences of the stimuli. Our initial and arbitrary choice of 33% as the proportion of "same" trials is responsible for this uncertainty in explanation — an uncertainty that will have to be resolved by subsequent research.

Nevertheless, it is clear that the differential effect of masking dot density over the ranges of the three tasks is greatly reduced if considered in this normalized context and the crossover of the detection and discrimination curves is probably best considered to be a secondary perturbation. The sequence in which the outcomes of the three experiments are ordered is also consistent with the idea that additional information is needed to progress from one of these perceptual tasks to the next and, therefore, a hierarchy of perceptual processes seemingly does exist.

Another major outcome of these three experiments concerns the effect of form on the three tasks. It had earlier been shown that the three-dimensional geometrical form of the dotted stimulus shapes (shown in Figure 6) only slightly affected *detectability* (See Figure 12 in Uttal, 1985) when stimuli are presented in this mixed set. Figure 12 plots the pooled results of this study for the three tasks as a function of stimulus-form with all data for all observers, all noise-dot densities, and all stimulus-form dot densities pooled. This figure clearly shows that this minimal insensitivity to form observed in the *detection* task also occurs when observers are asked to *discriminate* between these same forms. However, it is also immediately evident that there is an effect of stimulus form when the observers are asked to *recognize* the members of this set of stimuli. In particular, the paraboloid of rotation is recognized at higher levels than are the others, and the hemisphere and the two cubics form a second level of recognizability ease. The cylinder, plane, saddle, and parabolic arch can be clustered into a third, lower, and nearly equally recognizable group.

Unfortunately, this pattern of response in Experiment 3 as a function of stimulus-form is not replicated in the results of Experiment 6. Therefore, it is necessary to be somewhat cautious in accepting these data. Stimulus-form seems to remain a peculiar independent variable producing different results with different observers and/or different sets of stimuli. This is so in the recognition experiments in spite of the fact it produces little or no effect on the results from the discrimination and detection task experiments. The suggestion arises, therefore, that perhaps recognition is more dependent upon higher level cognitive differences than are discrimination or recognition. Recognition performance may be said to be more "cognitively" penetratable than is either of the other two visual processes.

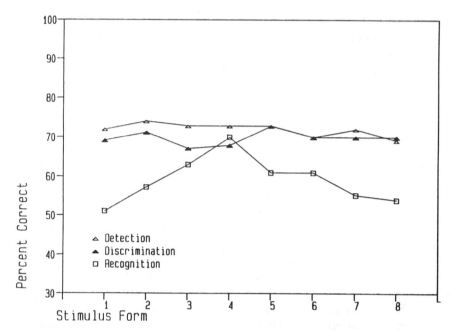

FIG. 12    The results of Experiment 1, 2, and 3 plotted as a function of the stimulus-form with task as a parameter. The effect of shape on recognition is not replicated in other experiments and is not considered to be a valid measure of performance in this case. See the discussion in the text on stimulus-set effects. The stimulus-forms are coded by the numbers on the horizontal axis in this graph and in all subsequent ones that plot data as a function of stimulus-form. 1 = cylinder; 2 = parabolic arch; 3 = hemisphere; 4 = paraboloid of rotation; 5 = cubic in one dimension; 6 = cubic in two dimensions; 7 = saddle; 8 = plane.

Figure 13 breaks some of this data down for the detection experiment. The three different densities of the stimulus-form pooled in Figure 12 have been separated to produce three curves that show that the negligible effect of form holds true across all three stimulus dot densities. This figure shows that there is no effect, other than a surprisingly moderate diminution of detectability, as the density of the stimulus-form is reduced. Obviously, this modest influence is, to a certain degree, an artifact due to the pooling of the data over the full range of masking dot densities that were utilized, some of which were not sufficiently dense to adequately mask the stimulus. However, it also suggests that the human visual system is very good at detecting these forms. To really determine the limits of its ability to do so, it will be necessary to push deeper into the realm of reduced stimulus-form densities to determine at what point the reconstruction process has insufficient information to carry out its function. This strategy will be the main theme of the next study in this series.

Figures 14 and 15 make the same comparison of the data as a function of stimulus-form dot density for the discrimination and recognition experiments, respectively. Again we see no qualitative change in the characteristic shape of the curves, simply a modest lowering of the absolute performance levels, as the density of the stimulus-form is decreased. Again the small effect of stimulus-form dot density is probably due to the pooling strategy used in our data analyses. Thus, it probably underestimates the true influence of stimulus-form dot density, a function more correctly shown in Figures 30, 31, 33, and 34.

The conclusion that stimulus-form exerts only a minimal effect in the discrimination experiment, however, may not be as simple and absolute as it seems at first inspection of the data. Because of the experimental design of this study, another form of analysis is also available to help demonstrate any subtle form effects that were not detectable in the raw data. Specifically, in the discrimination and the recognition experiments it is possible to collect confusion data and tabulate error matrices as a function of the specific discriminations or recognitions that were made. In this manner we were able to show which stimulus forms were confused with which others. As we shall see, there do appear to be subtle form effects reflected in the discrimination data as well as the recognition data when they are analyzed in this manner even

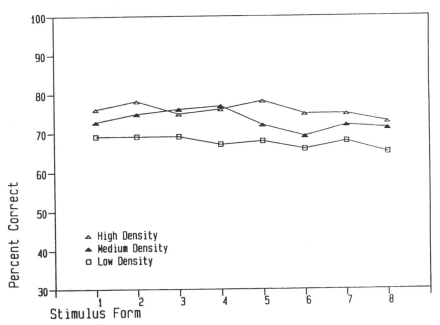

FIG. 13    The results of Experiment 1 — a study of *detection* — with the three densities of the stimulus-form as a parameter showing the absence of any differential form effect at any density.

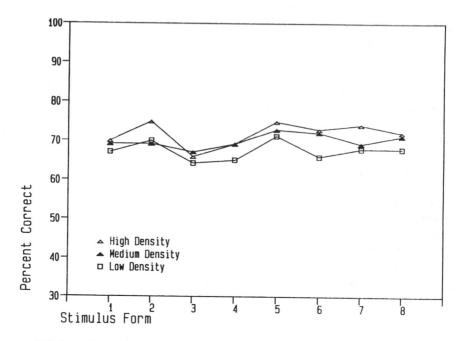

FIG. 14    The results of Experiment 2 — a study of *discrimination* — with the three densities of the stimulus-form as a parameter showing the absence of any differential form effect at any density.

though there is no sign of them in graphs plotting the raw performance as a function of stimulus-form.

The error matrix data[7] for the discrimination experiment are presented in Table 3.[8] To simplify this presentation, only error rates greater than 20% have been tabulated. The full error matrix is also presented in Table 4. These data are pooled across all three stimulus-form dot densities. The error matrix indicates situations in which *either* the two stimuli were the same but were reported to be different or in which they actually were different but were reported to be the same. In this cumulative error matrix, the results for all three stimulus-form dot densities have been aggregated into a single table. These data are tabulated as the percentage error rates for each of the 64 combinations of the eight different forms. A combination, it should be recalled, is the pairing of any one of the eight stimulus-forms (pooled across stimulus-form dot-density) with itself or any of the other seven in a two-presentation discrimination trial.

An examination of the error matrix shown in Tables 3 and 4 reveals a number of interesting features. First, the error rates tabulated in terms of the percentage of errors occurring in each cell for pairs that are identical does not systematically differ from those that are different. There are both higher and lower values of the error scores in the off-diagonal cells (where the observer

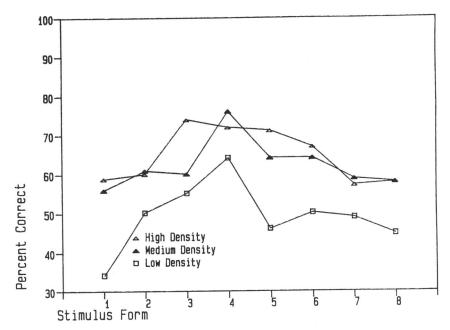

FIG. 15   The results of Experiment 3 — a study of recognition — with the three densities of the stimulus-form as a parameter showing a comparable differential form effect at all densities. But, see text for details.

---

[7]The data reported here for the correct and error discrimination matrices for the random stimuli were not actually collected in the course of Experiment 2. A computer malfunction unfortunately obliterated that portion of the data (the raw scores reported earlier were preserved). A set of equivalent data was collected during the course of Experiment 5 and is used in this discussion. The only difference in these scores is that they were not collected from the matched group of observers used throughout Experiments 1, 2, and 3. Since comparisons are made only within the context of these tables, it is believed that no significant biases of our interpretation are introduced by the substitution of these data for the lost set.

[8]It is very important for the reader to understand that the error matrices for the discrimination and recognition experiments, though superficially similar, do not have exactly the same meaning. First, the diagonal cells in the discrimination experiment designate the error rate when the two stimuli were the same but were reported by the observers to be different. The diagonal cells in the recognition experiment error matrix, on the other hand, indicate when the observer correctly identified the stimulus form. Second, the off-diagonal cells in the discrimination error matrices indicate the percentage of errors when the pair of stimulus-forms indicated by that cell was present. This percentage of errors was calculated by determining the number of erroneous responses and dividing it by the number of times that particular cell's designated combination of stimulus-forms was presented. In the recognition experiment on the other hand, the off-diagonal cells indicate the percentage of errors obtained by dividing the number of times the response designated by that cell erroneously occurred by the total number of times that that particular stimulus had been presented. In the recognition experiment on the other hand, the off-diagonal cells indicate the percentage of errors obtained by dividing the number of times the response designated by that cell erroneously occured by the total number of times that that particular stimulus had been presented.

TABLE 3

The error matrix for Experiment 5 — the *discrimination* experiment — (used in the discussion of Experiment 2). Scores in this table and in Tables 4 and 5 (a, b, and c) are tabulated as the percentage of errors of the total number of times a given stimulus-form pair (of the 64 possible combinations) was presented. The vertical columns need not add to 100%. Note the difference in meaning of the discrimination scores in these error matrices and those in the recognition error matrices. Only values greater than 20% have been shown to highlight the major interactions. Values in parentheses were deemed important and close enough to the threshold to be included.

| | CYL. | ARCH | HEMIS | PARBOLO. | CUBIC1D | CUBIC2D | SADDLE | PLANE |
|---|---|---|---|---|---|---|---|---|
| CYL. | 28.7 | 31.4 | | | | 22.4 | 30.5 | 20.5 |
| ARCH | 27.9 | 28.1 | | | | | 24.8 | |
| HEMIS | | | 24.7 | 25.0 | | | | |
| PARBOLO. | | | 25.3 | 28.0 | | | | |
| CUBIC1D | | | | | 28.1 | 32.6 | | |
| CUBIC2D | 23.8 | | | | 34.3 | 28.6 | 24.3 | 27.5 |
| SADDLE | 34.4 | 23.8 | | | | 24.2 | 28.8 | 23.0 |
| PLANE | (19.7) | | | | | 30.5 | 26.1 | 28.3 |

was asked if two nonidentical stimuli were the same or different) than on the diagonal cells (where the observer was asked if two identical stimuli were the same or different). There is no greater likelihood, in other words, that the same stimulus-form will be seen to be different any more or less often than different forms will be seen to be the same.

Another interesting aspect of this error matrix, however, is the fact that it is very symmetrical: The table exhibits a strongly diagonal symmetry. This is an internal check on the reliability of the data obtained in this experiment, because each cell is the equivalent of its diagonal pair. That is, the two cells in a diagonal pair represent exactly the same combination with but one exception — the order of the two stimulus forms is reversed in the sequential presentation of the trial. The fact that the matrix is so diagonally symmetrical suggests that there is no substantial sequence effect or response preference biasing our data and that the results are mainly attributed to the nature of the stimuli.

The fact that the scores in the cells on the diagonal axis of the table remain so constant (only one value deviates from the 28% error score exhibited by all other identical stimulus pairs by anything other than a third decimal place difference) confirms the fact that in this discrimination experiment, there is little influence of form on the performance of our observers in the conditions in which they are asked to discriminate the same form from itself. The absence of a stimulus-form effect on these raw percentage correct scores is also seen in Figures 12 and 14.

However, there is a very important result lurking in the complex error matrix tables. Indeed, it is the long sought stimulus-form effect itself. It can be

TABLE 4

The error matrix for Experiment 5 with all values shown.

|  | CYL. | ARCH | HEMIS | PARBOLO. | CUBIC1D | CUBIC2D | SADDLE | PLANE |
|---|---|---|---|---|---|---|---|---|
| CYL. | 28.7 | 31.4 | 10.6 | 9.1 | 15.6 | 22.4 | 30.5 | 20.5 |
| ARCH | 27.9 | 28.1 | 7.5 | 10.2 | 12.3 | 12.6 | 24.8 | 11.4 |
| HEMIS | 11.5 | 5.7 | 24.7 | 25.0 | 9.4 | 14.2 | 12.7 | 10.3 |
| PARBOLO. | 7.7 | 10.2 | 25.3 | 28.0 | 8.5 | 12.0 | 6.4 | 7.0 |
| CUBIC1D | 11.0 | 11.1 | 7.5 | 7.2 | 28.1 | 32.6 | 17.8 | 13.4 |
| CUBIC2D | 23.8 | 11.4 | 11.3 | 10.4 | 34.3 | 28.6 | 24.3 | 27.5 |
| SADDLE | 34.4 | 23.8 | 10.1 | 9.9 | 16.7 | 24.2 | 28.8 | 23.0 |
| PLANE | 19.7 | 10.9 | 14.9 | 7.3 | 13.5 | 30.5 | 26.1 | 28.3 |

detected in the subtle, but measurable, pattern of confusions that is seen in the other cells of the discrimination error matrix shown in Table 4. These confusions appear when the observer is asked to discriminate dissimilar pairs. There are, in fact, substantial differences among the error values displayed in this table in those cases. The differences are often substantial; note, for example, the range between the largest error rate (34.4% in cell "saddle-cylinder") and the lowest error rate (6.4% in cell "paraboloid-saddle"). This wide range of confusion scores indicates that there is an effect of form in this experiment that was not visible in the raw data plotted simply as the raw correct percentage as a function of the eight stimulus-forms. These data suggest that certain stimuli can be discriminated from certain other stimuli much more easily than can other stimulus pairs. Clearly the observers in this experiment found it much easier to discriminate between either the hemisphere and the paraboloid of rotation and any other form displayed in a trial presentation than between the hemisphere and paraboloid themselves.

Other combinations also show variations in the error scores, supporting the hypothesis that the geometric form of the items in a stimulus pair *does* play a significant role in the discriminability task (and, as we shall also see, in the recognition experiment). As specific examples, our observers were able to easily discriminate between an arch and a surface (values of the error cells reprsenting the comparisons being 10.9% and 11.4%, respectively). On the other hand, the cylinder was very often confused with the saddle (error rate = 34.3%). In sum, if we use a 20% confusion criterion, the main clusters of confusion in the discrimination experiments with randomly sampled stimuli are:

1. The arch, the cylinder, the two-dimensional cubic, and the saddle.
2. The hemisphere and the paraboloid of rotation.
3. The one-dimensional cubic and the two-dimensional cubic.
4. The two-dimensional cubic is also confused with the cylinder, the saddle, and the plane. *But they are not confused with the one-dimensional cubic.*

However, if we had used a slightly higher (25%) criterion, it would be noted that the strongest clusters occur between:

1. The cylinder, arch, and saddle.
2. The hemisphere and the paraboloid of rotation.
3. The one-dimensional cubic and the two dimensional cubic (with the plane being confused with the latter but not the former).

These stronger associations are highlighted by the fact that this is exactly the same strong pattern of confusions observed in the recognition experiment —

an experiment that used a different set of observers! The confusion matrices, therefore, are remarkably stable across tasks and observers.[9]

The three parts of Table 5 shows the same data presented in Tables 3 and 4 but factored out for the three different stimulus-form densities. No great differences in the now apparent form effects as a function of density are present if one compares these tables with each other or with the composite Table 4.

The cumulative error matrix for the recognition experiment is shown in Table 6. In this tabulation each off-diagonal item in the table indicates the proportion of the trials that our observers responded with the name of a form other than that of the particular stimulus-form presented. To simplify this table, only those confusion values greater than 10% have been tabulated.

Several important outcomes of this experiment are also indicated by the data presented in this table. One of particular salience is, once again, the diagonal symmetry that is displayed by this table. This has the same significance as the diagonal symmetry in the discrimination error matrix. That is, response-forms that are confused with particular stimulus-forms are likely to be reciprocally confused with the same forms when presented as stimuli. Thus we see:

1. The cylinder and the arch being confused with the saddle.
2. The hemisphere and the paraboloid of rotation being strongly and reciprocally confused with each other.
3. The two-dimensional cubic being confused with the plane and the one-dimensional cubic with relatively high levels of reciprocal confusion, but the one-dimensional cubic is not confused with the plane.

It is interesting to note that these clusters do contain exactly the same stimuli as the clusters observed in the discrimination experiment and shown in Table 3 if one considers the higher (25%) criterion in Table 3.

Table 7 presents the confusion error results for recognition with the values of all cells entered. A more detailed analysis of the recognition data can be obtained by factoring apart the data for the three stimulus-form dot densities and presenting them in the tripartite Table 8. In this case, also, all of the data entries in the three matrices have been preserved. Close examination of these tables shows some modest deviations from the grand averages of Table 6, but it is clear that the same general pattern of confusions obtains at all three stimulus-form dot densities.

It is important to reiterate one important conclusion that emerges from the strong diagonal symmetry observed in Table 3 and Table 7. That conclusion

---

[9]However, in a manner confirming the general rule that slight changes produce big differences, it has subsequently been determined that there are other comparable stimulus-set conditions and tasks (e.g., construction from sparsely sampled dots) that produce other clusters. This work will be reported in a subsequent publication.

TABLE 5

The error matrices for the three levels of stimulus-form densities used in Experiment 5 — the *discrimination* experiment — factored apart in order to determine if there is any effect of this variable on the error matrices. According to these three matrices, there are no important shifts in the results as a function of the number of dots in the stimulus form. (a) The error matrix for stimuli containing 64 and 50 dots; (b) 49 and 38 dots; (c) 36 and 28 dots. See text for an explanation of these dual numbers.

|          | CYL. | ARCH | HEMIS | PARBOLO. | CUBIC1D | CUBIC2D | SADDLE | PLANE |
|----------|------|------|-------|----------|---------|---------|--------|-------|
| CYL.     | 28.0 | 28.6 | 9.2   | 9.0      | 12.9    | 16.6    | 29.7   | 16.9  |
| ARCH     | 28.8 | 27.6 | 5.1   | 15.8     | 11.7    | 10.2    | 23.0   | 6.3   |
| HEMIS    | 7.4  | 4.2  | 19.9  | 18.5     | 4.2     | 1.4     | 6.4    | 7.9   |
| PARBOLO. | 5.3  | 8.0  | 19.9  | 26.5     | 5.5     | 8.2     | 4.5    | 6.4   |
| CUBIC1D  | 7.9  | 8.2  | 2.8   | 5.1      | 24.3    | 21.7    | 13.4   | 8.5   |
| CUBIC2D  | 22.0 | 11.8 | 8.5   | 6.1      | 30.6    | 27.2    | 15.9   | 23.1  |
| SADDLE   | 29.7 | 20.5 | 8.2   | 9.6      | 10.1    | 21.7    | 26.2   | 21.3  |
| PLANE    | 20.6 | 9.7  | 10.5  | 5.6      | 13.9    | 21.7    | 17.3   | 24.9  |

(a)

|          | CYL. | ARCH | HEMIS | PARBOLO. | CUBIC1D | CUBIC2D | SADDLE | PLANE |
|----------|------|------|-------|----------|---------|---------|--------|-------|
| CYL.     | 29.6 | 30.6 | 8.0   | 7.8      | 11.1    | 18.0    | 26.4   | 19.8  |
| ARCH     | 21.8 | 27.4 | 6.4   | 5.9      | 8.2     | 8.4     | 16.0   | 11.0  |
| HEMIS    | 11.1 | 7.1  | 24.2  | 20.0     | 9.7     | 11.4    | 6.1    | 10.6  |
| PARBOLO. | 6.3  | 8.9  | 25.7  | 25.7     | 9.7     | 10.6    | 7.0    | 5.9   |
| CUBIC1D  | 12.7 | 11.1 | 8.5   | 7.4      | 29.1    | 28.5    | 14.1   | 12.3  |
| CUBIC2D  | 21.8 | 8.0  | 8.9   | 13.4     | 30.1    | 29.5    | 20.9   | 24.1  |
| SADDLE   | 27.4 | 23.1 | 6.0   | 5.9      | 7.0     | 19.9    | 29.7   | 22.3  |
| PLANE    | 15.4 | 10.5 | 15.4  | 6.2      | 13.4    | 30.8    | 22.1   | 27.3  |

(b)

|          | CYL. | ARCH | HEMIS | PARBOLO. | CUBIC1D | CUBIC2D | SADDLE | PLANE |
|----------|------|------|-------|----------|---------|---------|--------|-------|
| CYL.     | 28.5 | 34.1 | 14.1  | 10.8     | 19.3    | 29.0    | 34.1   | 24.5  |
| ARCH     | 33.5 | 30.5 | 10.8  | 11.1     | 17.0    | 18.5    | 30.1   | ·19.5 |
| HEMIS    | 18.2 | 9.7  | 29.2  | 33.7     | 11.5    | 18.0    | 24.1   | 17.4  |
| PARBOLO. | 12.1 | 13.1 | 30.4  | 31.5     | 10.2    | 18.4    | 7.4    | 9.3   |
| CUBIC1D  | 12.3 | 17.7 | 12.8  | 10.3     | 30.8    | 41.4    | 21.2   | 19.6  |
| CUBIC2D  | 30.5 | 17.9 | 16.2  | 17.2     | 44.8    | 28.9    | 30.5   | 34.7  |
| SADDLE   | 43.0 | 27.0 | 16.2  | 12.5     | 29.3    | 34.3    | 30.4   | 25.1  |
| PLANE    | 24.1 | 13.3 | 18.5  | 14.1     | 10.6    | 38.9    | 32.0   | 30.9  |

(c)

TABLE 6

The error matrix for Experiment 3 — the *recognition* experiment. Only values greater than 10% have been tabulated to highlight the major interactions.

|          | CYL. | ARCH | HEMIS | PARBOLO. | CUBIC1D | CUBIC2D | SADDLE | PLANE |
|----------|------|------|-------|----------|---------|---------|--------|-------|
| CYL.     | 51.1 | 13.3 |       |          |         |         | 12.2   |       |
| ARCH     | 10.5 | 57.6 |       |          |         |         | 14.7   |       |
| HEMIS    |      |      | 62.6  | 16.9     |         |         |        |       |
| PARBOLO. |      |      | 14.7  | 70.3     |         |         |        |       |
| CUBIC1D  |      |      |       |          | 61.3    | 9.7     |        |       |
| CUBIC2D  |      |      |       |          | 23.1    | 60.8    |        | 15.1  |
| SADDLE   | 12.8 | 14.3 |       |          |         |         | 54.6   |       |
| PLANE    |      |      |       |          |         | 10.5    |        | 54.3  |

## TABLE 7

The error matrix for Experiment 3—the recognition experiment—with all values shown. For Tables 7 and 8 (a, b, and c) the error scores shown in the off-diagonal cells are tabulated as the percent of the total numbers of times the stimulus in that column was presented. The scores in each vertical column should sum to 100% plus or minus a small rounding error. The diagonal cells are the correct responses and do not indicate errors. They correspond to the values shown for recognition in Figure 12 for Table 7 and in Figure 15 for Tables 8a, b, and c. Note the difference in meaning of these scores and those for the discrimination error matrices.

|          | CYL. | ARCH | HEMIS | PARBOLO. | CUBIC1D | CUBIC2D | SADDLE | PLANE |
|----------|------|------|-------|----------|---------|---------|--------|-------|
| CYL.     | 51.1 | 13.3 | 3.8   | 1.4      | 2.4     | 4.6     | 12.2   | 8.5   |
| ARCH     | 10.5 | 57.6 | 1.9   | 1.6      | 2.2     | 2.2     | 14.7   | 2.9   |
| HEMIS    | 5.2  | 3.5  | 62.6  | 16.9     | 2.8     | 4.7     | 3.3    | 6.3   |
| PARBOLO. | 2.7  | 2.4  | 14.7  | 70.3     | 1.4     | 2.8     | 2.6    | 2.7   |
| CUBIC1D  | 2.3  | 2.0  | 2.2   | 1.4      | 61.3    | 9.7     | 2.5    | 3.4   |
| CUBIC2D  | 7.1  | 4.6  | 6.6   | 4.1      | 23.1    | 60.8    | 6.7    | 15.1  |
| SADDLE   | 12.8 | 14.3 | 3.4   | 2.4      | 3.7     | 4.6     | 54.6   | 6.9   |
| PLANE    | 8.4  | 2.3  | 4.7   | 1.7      | 3.0     | 10.5    | 3.4    | 54.3  |

## TABLE 8

The error matrices for the three different levels of stimulus-form density used in Experiment 3 — the *recognition* experiment — factored apart to determine if there was any effect of this variable on the recognition of the eight forms. When compared with Table 7, it is obvious that there are no important differences between the results at any of the three levels. (a) The error matrix for stimuli using 64 and 50 dots; (b) 49 and 38 dots; (c) 36 and 28 dots.

|           | CYL. | ARCH | HEMIS | PARBOLO. | CUBIC1D | CUBIC2D | SADDLE | PLANE |
|-----------|------|------|-------|----------|---------|---------|--------|-------|
| CYL.      | 59.3 | 17.6 | 2.0   | 1.0      | 2.3     | 3.8     | 11.2   | 8.8   |
| ARCH      | 7.6  | 60.1 | 1.4   | 1.4      | 1.6     | 1.5     | 16.8   | 2.9   |
| HEMIS     | 4.3  | 2.9  | 73.7  | 18.6     | 1.6     | 4.1     | 2.4    | 6.4   |
| PARBOLO.  | 2.8  | 2.3  | 11.4  | 72.2     | 0.6     | 1.9     | 2.3    | 2.7   |
| CUBIC1D   | 1.7  | 1.5  | 1.2   | 1.1      | 70.8    | 8.6     | 2.3    | 3.1   |
| CUBIC2D   | 5.6  | 2.6  | 4.1   | 3.0      | 19.4    | 67.2    | 5.8    | 12.8  |
| SADDLE    | 12.6 | 11.6 | 2.6   | 1.6      | 1.8     | 3.9     | 57.2   | 4.8   |
| PLANE     | 6.2  | 1.5  | 3.7   | 1.1      | 2.0     | 9.0     | 2.0    | 58.6  |

(a)

73

|          | CYL. | ARCH | HEMIS | PARBOLO. | CUBIC1D | CUBIC2D | SADDLE | PLANE |
|----------|------|------|-------|----------|---------|---------|--------|-------|
| CYL.     | 56.7 | 9.6  | 3.8   | 0.7      | 2.1     | 3.8     | 14.1   | 9.4   |
| ARCH     | 8.0  | 61.5 | 1.6   | 1.4      | 1.7     | 1.9     | 13.0   | 2.1   |
| HEMIS    | 4.7  | 3.4  | 60.3  | 15.0     | 2.9     | 4.3     | 2.6    | 4.8   |
| PARBOLO. | 2.4  | 2.1  | 17.9  | 76.1     | 1.5     | 1.8     | 1.6    | 2.1   |
| CUBIC1D  | 2.2  | 2.4  | 2.4   | 1.2      | 64.1    | 9.4     | 1.9    | 2.7   |
| CUBIC2D  | 6.7  | 4.4  | 7.3   | 2.6      | 21.6    | 64.1    | 5.1    | 13.9  |
| SADDLE   | 12.0 | 14.0 | 3.4   | 2.0      | 3.8     | 3.6     | 58.8   | 6.7   |
| PLANE    | 7.1  | 2.2  | 3.3   | 0.8      | 2.5     | 11.0    | 2.9    | 58.3  |

(b)

74

|          | CYL.  | ARCH | HEMIS | PARBOLO. | CUBIC1D | CUBIC2D | SADDLE | PLANE |
|----------|-------|------|-------|----------|---------|---------|--------|-------|
| CYL.     | 33.9  | 12.1 | 5.6   | 2.4      | 3.0     | 6.3     | 11.7   | 7.2   |
| ARCH     | 17.1  | 50.0 | 2.8   | 2.1      | 3.4     | 3.3     | 14.1   | 3.4   |
| HEMIS    | 6.85  | 4.4  | 54.9  | 17.1     | 4.5     | 5.8     | 4.6    | 7.8   |
| PARBOLO. | 2.8   | 2.8  | 14.3  | 63.8     | 2.4     | 4.8     | 3.8    | 3.4   |
| CUBIC1D  | 3.3   | 2.3  | 3.0   | 1.9      | 46.1    | 11.3    | 3.2    | 4.4   |
| CUBIC2D  | 9.37  | 7.4  | 8.2   | 6.5      | 29.6    | 50.2    | 8.7    | 19.2  |
| SADDLE   | 13.8  | 17.9 | 4.1   | 3.4      | 6.1     | 6.4     | 48.8   | 9.9   |
| PLANE    | 12.7  | 3.6  | 7.2   | 3.0      | 4.9     | 11.9    | 5.2    | 44.5  |

(c)

is that it is unlikely that any very strong response preference or bias was at work in this part of this study just as it was also absent in the discrimination experiment study. The data, to the contrary, speak to a system of responses that are driven more by the nature of the stimulus than by any predilection on the part of the observer to respond with any particular stimulus-form name. While this result emphasizes the preattentive, precognitive influences that dominate performance in the experimental tasks used in this study, it does not entirely preclude some cognitive influence on the other aspects of the responses generated by our observers.

## Experiment 4

Experiment 4 was designed to replicate the comparison of random and regularly sampled stimuli in the detection task originally carried out and reported in the most recent of the previous monographs (Uttal, 1984). The replication was not exact, however, since the set of eight stimulus-forms that have been used throughout this study were used in this experiment. In the original 1984 study, the comparison had been made between random and regular versions of a single stimulus-form (in each experiment) that varied in both dot density

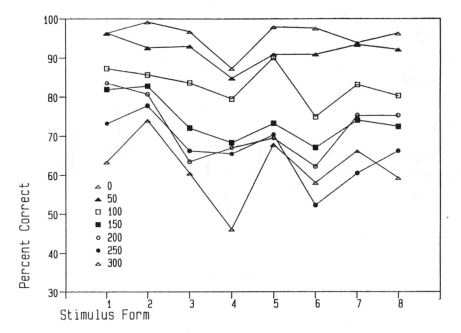

FIG. 16   The results of the first part of Experiment 4 in which observers were asked to *detect* randomly sampled forms. The data are parametric across the seven masking dot densities and plotted as a function of the eight stimulus-forms.

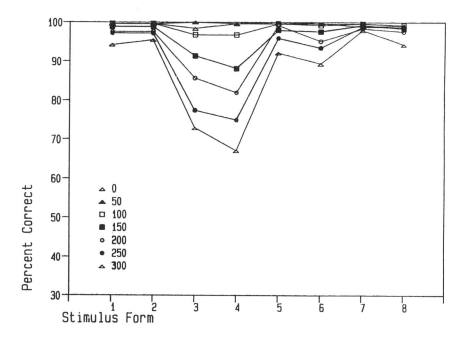

FIG. 17    The results of the second part of Experiment 4 in which observers were asked to *detect* regularly sampled forms. The data are parametric across the seven masking dot densities and are plotted as function of the eight stimulus-forms.

and degree of stretch from a plane to the most extremely distorted version of that particular form. The two experiments are, therefore, not entirely identical. Some conditions are identical in the earlier and in the present experiment and these cross-referencing conditions do allow us to at least partially compare the relative effects of regular and random forms respectively.

The results of this fourth experiment are shown in Figures 16 through 19. Figures 16 and 17 show the raw data for this study displayed as a function of the shape of the stimulus and parametric in terms of the masking dot density for random and regular forms respectively. Figure 18 pools the data from these raw results as a function of stimulus-form into a summary across all masking dot density levels, while Figure 19 plots these same data, but in this case pooled across forms and plotted as a function of the masking dot density.

It is clear that what we had previously believed to be a solid law of dotted form perception — The Rule of Random Sampling — does not hold under the conditions of this experiment. In this case there is a clear cut superiority of detection for the regularly sampled forms over the randomly sampled ones. Furthermore, there is, among the regularly sampled stimuli, a superiority of the linear regular arrays over those generated from a decagonal prototype.

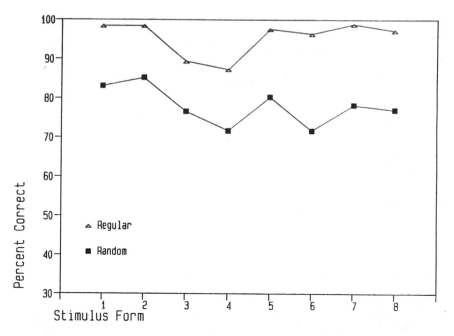

FIG. 18   The results of both parts of Experiment 4 (in which the task was *detection*) pooled and plotted as a function of the eight stimulus-forms.

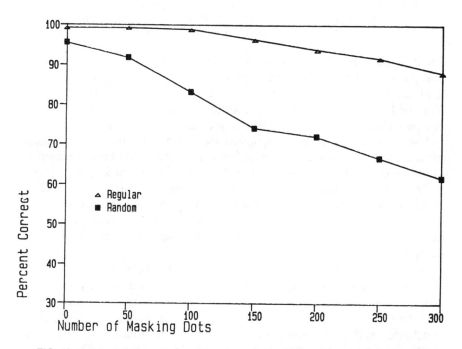

FIG. 19   The results of both parts of Experiment 4 pooled and plotted as a function of the number of masking dots.

The discrepancy between the older results showing the superiority of random sampled stimuli over regularly sampled ones and the present ones showing, conversely, the superiority of the regularly sampled ones over the randomly sampled ones is discussed in Appendix A.

The data presented in Figures 16 and 17 and in the summary Figure 18 display a substantial detection deficit for the hemisphere and the paraboloid of rotation when they are generated from the regularly sampled prototypes, and a more modest deficit, in addition to one for the two-dimensional cubic, when they are sampled from the randomly sampled prototypes. Surprisingly, this did not affect the discrimination data, as we shall shortly see.

## Experiment 5

Experiment 5 was designed to compare the discriminability of regular and randomly sampled forms, unlike Experiment 2, which dealt only with randomly sampled forms. The results of this experiment for the standard set of eight random forms are shown in Figure 20. In this figure the data have been presented as a function of the eight stimulus-forms and are parametric in terms of the noise dot density. Only the medium level of stimulus-form dot

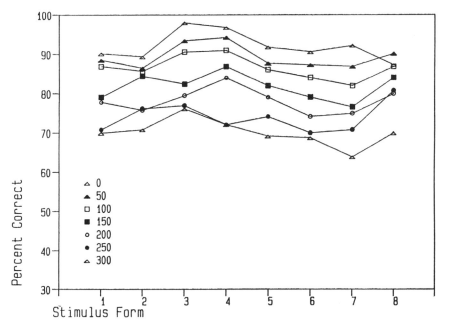

FIG. 20    The results of the first part of Experiment 5 in which the observers were asked to *discriminate* between pairs of randomly sampled forms. The data are parametric across the seven masking dot densities and plotted as a function of the eight stimulus-forms.

density has been tabulated here. (The results for the high and low density values, though collected simultaneously, are not summarized here). The equivalent, medium density, data for the regular stimuli are shown in Figure 21 analyzed in the same way. Figure 22 pools the data obtained for the medium density stimulus values across all three masking dot densities to more clearly illustrate the difference between the responses to the two kinds of sampling. Figure 23 pools the data across all of the forms and plots them as a function of the masking dot density. In neither case was there any differential effect of stimulus form at the three stimulus-form dot densities used in this experiment.

The main point in this outcome of the comparison of these two sets of stimuli lies in the absolute performance levels displayed by the observers (who were the same in each of the two parts of this experiment). It is clear, in this case, that the regularly sampled stimuli are also discriminated significantly better than are the randomly sampled stimuli regardless of which stimulus-form is compared with which. A secondary outcome of this first level of analysis is that, unlike the detection case, these data exhibit only a very modest effect of stimulus-form. Figures 20 and 21 compare the form ef-

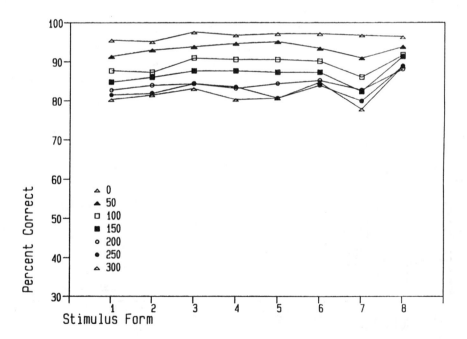

FIG. 21    The results of the second part of Experiment 5 in which the observers were asked to *discriminate* between pairs of regularly sampled forms. The data are parametric across the seven masking dot densities and plotted as a function of the stimulus-form.

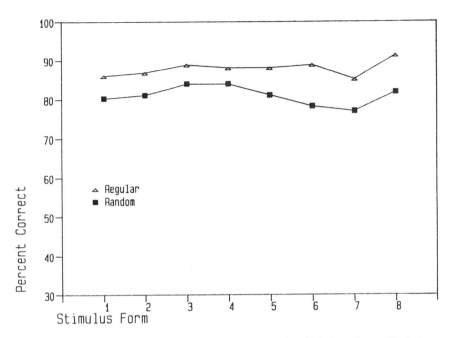

FIG. 22 The results of both parts of Experiment 5 (in which the task was *discrimination*) pooled and plotted as function of the stimulus-form.

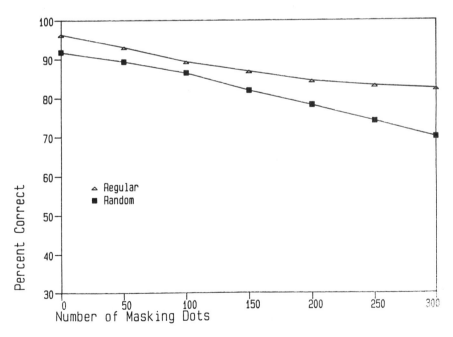

FIG. 23 The results of both parts of Experiment 5 pooled and plotted as a function of the number of masking dots.

fect across the three different levels of stimulus-form dot density for the ran--dom and regular stimuli respectively. No important deviation in the performance of the response as a function of form can be observed.

### Experiment 6

Experiment 6 was designed to compare the influence of random and regular stimulus-forms on the recognition task. The results of the experiment are shown in Figures 24 through 27. Figures 24 and 25 show the results for the set of medium density stimuli that were used in this comparison for the randomly sampled and regularly sampled stimuli, respectively. Because of the relatively modest number of trials that have been pooled in each of these two parts of this experiment (typically we use three times the numbers of trials), the data fluctuate somewhat more than is typical, but the main points are clear enough. Random forms are much less recognizable than are regular ones in the context of this experiment. Indeed, the range of masking dot densities used to effectively mask stimulus-forms generated from random

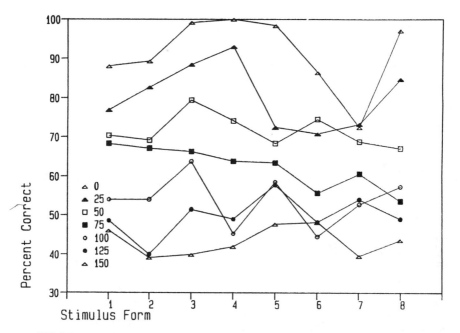

FIG. 24    The results of the first part of Experiment 6 in which the observers were asked to *recognize* randomly sampled forms. The data are parametric across the seven masking dot densities and plotted as a function of the eight stimulus-forms. Note that in this case the range of masking dot numerosity is smaller than in the other experiments, varying from 0 to 150 rather than from 0 to 300.

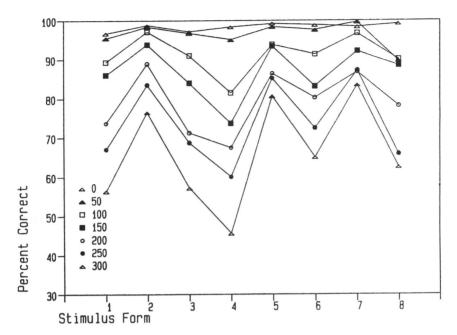

FIG. 25    The results of the second part of Experiment 6 in which the observers were asked to *recognize* regularly sampled forms. The data are parametric across the seven masking dot densities used and plotted as a function the eight stimulus-forms.

samples was only half that required to mask regular forms. (Note that the range of the parameter of masking dot densities used differs in these two graphs.)

Figure 26 shows these data for both the randomly and regularly sampled stimulus-forms pooled across all masking dot densities plotted on the same graph. The advantages of the regularly sampled forms are even more clearly depicted in this figure. This figure, however, displays an unsystematic pattern of responses to the different forms, unlike the systematic results that were obtained in Experiment 3, which were plotted in Figure 12.

Thus, there is a strong effect of regularity and randomness exhibited in this experiment — stimuli generated by the former strategy being much more recognizable than these generated by the latter. This same point is also made by examining Figure 27 in which the performance is plotted for both parts of the experiment as a function of the masking dot density per se. On the other hand, because of the rather modest numbers of trials in the two parts of this experiment, we have had to dig deeper to see the effect of stimulus-form, an effect that only became evident in the error matrices but that was invisible in the raw data. This analysis has already been tabulated for the random stimui in Tables 6, 7, and 8 and discussed earlier.

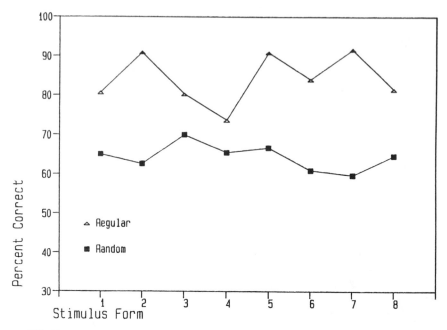

FIG. 26    The results of both parts of Experiment 6 (in which the task was recognition) pooled and plotted as a function of the eight stimulus-forms.

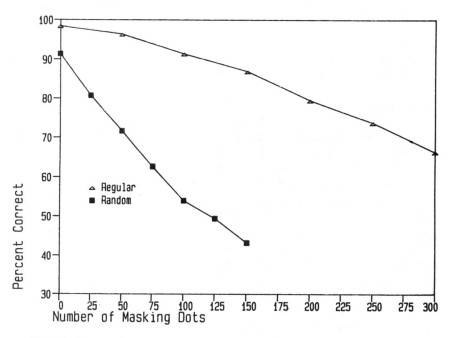

FIG. 27    The results of both parts of Experiment 7 pooled and plotted as a function of the number of masking dots.

84

## Experiment 7

Experiment 7 was mainly designed as a control to guarantee that the negligible influence of form that was repeatedly observed in this study was not due to an obscure artifact associated with cueing by local areas. An often suggested criticism of this conclusion was that there was no form effect detected because our observers used small, local regions that were nearly flat even on the curved surfaces, to cue the detection, discrimination, or recognition of the stimulus-forms. The outcome of this experiment substantiated the observation that, quite to the contrary of this putative criticism, the objective two-dimensional density determined detectability rather than subjective density and that, in fact, observers were not sensitive to the apparent three-dimensional shapes of the stimulus-form we utilized in these studies.

As in previous experiments, detectability improved in this control experiment with increased numbers of dots in the planar stimulus-form and declined with increased numbers of masking dots. This is the measured effect of the signal-to-noise ratio of the real dot densities. Of primary interest in this experiment, however, was the relation between detectability and variations in the apparent orientation and, thus, subjective density of a stimulus plane placed within a rectangular parallelopiped. This outcome is plotted in Figure

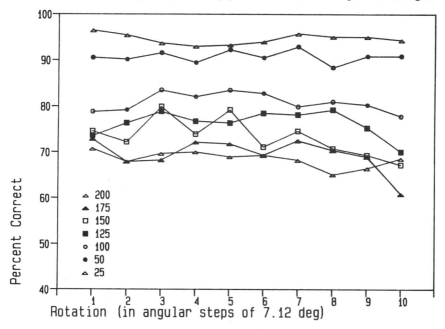

FIG. 28    The results of Experiment 7 plotted as a function of the angle of rotation at which the plane was oriented in a given trial. Obviously there is no effect of orientation and, therefore, of the apparent density of the plane.

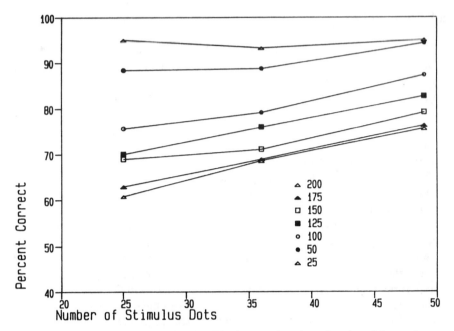

FIG. 29   The results of Experiment 7. The data are plotted as a function of the number of dots in the stimulus-form and are parametric across the number of masking dots.

28, for the seven different masking dot densities. In this figure the results for 25, 36, and 49 stimulus-form dot densities are pooled. It is immediately apparent that any effect of orientation upon detectability must be extremely small. The same data, pooled across orientations, is plotted in Figure 29 as a function of the number of dots in the stimulus plane.

These results resemble those obtained for curved surfaces in showing insensitivity to apparent departures of a stereoscopically generated surface from a fronto-parallel plane. However, questions, doubts, and criticisms that can be raised in connection with the curved surfaces do not apply to stimuli designed as they are in the present experiment. The obtained results, therefore, are more clear cut in their implications. Because the apparent density of the dots in the stimulus plane varied by more than 2 to 1 (for a given number of dots) as the plane shifted from the fronto-parallel to the diagonal position (thus varying its apparent surface area), we should have observed substantially reduced detectability scores. The lack of such a trend suggests that the apparent third dimension does not combine with the other two in an Euclidean fashion in this context. Our confidence is thus raised that the shape effects are small or idiosyncratic in detection for real visual information processing rather than for artifactual reasons.

# 5 Discussion

This study of the detectability, discriminability, and recognizability of regular and randomly sampled geometric forms is an exploration into the psychophysical properties of the mainly preattentive, perceptual processing of the gestalt or global properties of a particular set of dotted, discrete, sampled stimulus-forms. As the many qualifying adjectives and other equivocating terms of the previous sentence suggest, the goals of this study are quite limited. The general relevance of this work to other kinds of visual perception (other than dotted forms) is constrained by the abstract nature of the sparsely sampled arrays that have been utilized as stimulus-forms and the narrow range of responses allowed observers in the experiments. In order to make our experiments both psychophysically and mathematically tractable, a relatively simple and greatly reduced abstract stimulus was "gracefully degraded" from realistic scenes by randomly sampling discrete points on certain well defined geometrical shapes. This procedure has the effect of emphasizing the properties of the observer's processing of the organizational and molar attributes of the stimulus as opposed to any local features of which it may be composed. The reason for this is simple: Dotted forms of the kind used in this study contain no local features. At the theoretical level, it also forces us towards a holistic, rather than an elementalistic, interpretation of the results.

In order to make the task challenging to our observers' otherwise spectacularly competent visual systems, we have added controlled amounts of random dots to each stimulus display as a degrading mask. This was done as an alternative to, but the technique plays the same role as, reducing the contrast of a grating or the focus of an image — that of controlled image degradation. Because of this extreme simplification from realistic scenes, our experimental controls are precise and the opportunities for plausible and useful analyses greatly extended. Because of the discrete nature of the sampled (dotted) stimulus-forms that have been utilized in the psychophysical experiments, it has been possible specifically to test an array of formal computer modeling techniques that would either be computationally prohibitive or unformulizable in the context of the analysis of continuous scenes. Nevertheless, even as narrowly defined as this research program was intended to be, it still turned out to be the case that the obtained psychophysical results described a system of visual processes of great complexity and most of the computer models were too simple to represent the results. The goals of this discussion section are to tease out some order from the results, to establish general rules of psychophysical performance, and to develop, to the extent possible, some informal mathematical statements concerning the three kinds of perception of dotted forms studied here. As shall become increasingly evident, only partial attainment of these goals has been achieved.

In the past, analytic approaches to modeling the psychophysical data have had both successes and failures: In two dimensions, an autocorrelational model (Uttal, 1975) was a powerful predictor of psychophysical performance in detection experiments. In three dimensions, the successes have so far been fewer and further between. In particular, detection in three dimensions was not well predicted by a simple-minded extrapolation of autocorrelation from the two-dimensional version of the model, nor have discrimination and recognition been adequately modeled by analogous cross correlation algorithms. Although the difficulty with the autocorrelation model has been partially ameliorated by our recantations of the hypothesis that randomly sampled stimulus-forms are detected better than regularly sampled ones – a very discrepant result – the repeated demonstration that the degree of three-dimensional stretch does not influence performance in any of the three tasks is sufficient to invalidate a simplistic correlational interpretation of these results a priori.

My general approach has been to use analytic methods rather than statistical ones. There are several important aspects of this kind of analytic modeling that should be made explicit. First, unlike the statistical approach, the analytic approach is deterministic. It deals with specific stimulus-forms rather than probabilistically defined ones and stimulus-driven responses rather than subjectively varying response biases. It thus stresses the stimulus determination of performance rather than any aspect of decisions or response selection. Because of the generally preattentive nature of the processes that we believe we are assaying here, this seems to be a more plausible approach and promises to provide the foundation for a more intuitively satisfying and realistic theoretical explanation of our psychophysical data than some of the more statistical models that have been used in the past.

The decision to pursue this analytic line of theoretical analysis is not without its metatheoretical commitments. Combined with the preattentive and automatic philosophy that permeates the thinking of most of us in this subfield of visual perception research, a model of a passive, neural-network-like, computational engine quickly emerges concerning the nature of the mental processes underlying the phenomena that have been measured here. Whether this is correct or not is moot, and certainly other theoretical psychologists, such as Triesman (1982) and Triesman and Gelade (1980) dote more on the cognitive aspects of some of the same visual processes than on the automatic, preattentive ones emphasized here. Furthermore, there have been recurrent hints in our results of some vague kinds of "cognitive" influences on our data (e.g., interobserver differences, the influence of the stimulus set, etc.) that seem to suggest that the response is not solely a function of the isolated stimulus. Rather, some of these "low-level, preattentive" mechanisms seem to be "cognitively penetrable," at the very least.

Second, although the algorithms that are used to carry out this theoretical modeling effort are executed on a serial computer, in fact they are intrinsically parallel processes. That is, they describe mechanisms that can easily — in fact, most easily — be conceptualized in terms of parallel processing networks of the kind that are believed to be present in the human visual nervous system. There is an a priori face validity and intrinsic neuroreducationism to this type of model, therefore, in an anatomic and physiological sense that is not present in elaborate statistical explanations of form vision.

Our main task in this section is to test several putative mathematical models and theories by transforming the stimuli used in the psychophysical experiments just reported. We do so by using some of the analytic techniques mentioned above. (Our attempts are mentioned even in those cases in which they failed.) A more immediate goal, however, is necessary to lay the foundation for that theoretical task. I now summarize the psychophysical results that have been obtained.

## A SUMMARY OF RESULTS

1. Detection, discrimination and, recognition appear to be generally organized into a hierarchy in which successively higher amounts of information are required to overcome the degrading effects of masking random noise dots.

2. In a few exceptional conditions, typically at high masking dot densities, discrimination sometimes occurs at lower signal-to-noise ratios than does detection.

3. Detection and discrimination performance both appear to be relatively uninfluenced by the shape of the surface in terms fo their raw scores. Recognition scores are idiosyncratically influenced by stimulus shape varying with

observer groups and stimulus set. Both discrimination and recognition, however, do show a very reliable sensitivity to form in the error matrices for the various combinations that must be discriminated or the confusion errors in the recognition task.

4. The errors of discrimination and of recognition indicated in the error matrices are strongly diagonally symmetrical, indicating that no significant response bias occurs and that the responses are largely stimulus driven.

5. Detection, discrimination, and recognition data both show a prepotency of the regularly sampled forms over the randomly sampled one. When the standard set of eight stimulus-forms are presented intermixed, replications of earlier experiments show that the "Rule of Random Sampling" (in which single random forms appeared to be detected better than regular ones) was incorrect. (See Appendix A).

6. In the discrimination experiment with random stimuli, certain confusions (i.e., poor discriminations) occurred. The strongest ones are:
   a. The cylinder was difficult to discriminate from the arch and the saddle.
   b. The hemisphere and the paraboloid of rotation could not easily be discriminated from each other, but were quite discriminable from all others.
   c. The two-dimensional cubic was difficult to discriminate from the one-dimensional cubic and the plane, but the one-dimensional cubic was easily discriminated from the plane.

7. In the recognition experiment, using random stimuli, the pattern of results was virtually identical to the strongest confusions in the discrimination experiment, but the differences between the first and second tier of error scores was greater in recognition than in discrimination.
   a. The cylinder, arch, and saddle were confused with each other.
   b. The hemisphere and paraboloid were confused with each other.
   c. The one-dimensional cubic and the two-dimensional cubic were frequently confused and the two-dimensional cubic (but not the one-dimensional cubic) was confused with the plane.

8. When an elastic plane is rotated to different positions in a rectangular space, it does not vary in detectability in spite of the fact that there is a greater than two-to-one variation in its apparent dot density. This result negates any possibility that local region effects can account for the null effect of stimulus-form in the raw correct percentage graphs.

At this point, I would like to deal with one perplexing and continuing problem. Throughout this entire program of research, it has repeatedly been the case that experiments in which mixed groups of different stimulus-forms (i.e., different geometrical shapes — not different degrees of distortion) have been used, we have obtained inconsistent results when the findings are plotted as a function of the stimulus-form. Experiments that are nearly the same reflect different shape or form functions. Furthermore, observers behave quite idiosyncratically (i.e., they exhibit stronger individual differences) when faced with, for example, the eight different standard forms (utilized throughout the present work) rather than a single form varying in density or degree of deformation. In other words, when mixed sets of stimulus-forms are used and the response patterns of individual observers are compared, they typically do not show the same pattern of sensitivities to shape.[10]

Experiments of this kind, therefore, produce results that often are not comparable *when the data are analyzed as a function of the raw stimulus-form dimension* even though other measures and conditions are typically quite reliable and constant from one experimental situation to another. For example, in Experiments 3 and 6 we saw how the pattern of responses varied when simply plotted as a function of form even though the experimental situation was nearly identical. Error matrices, however, were comparable.

The problem seems to lie in the individual differences of the observer's responses to the specific stimulus-forms used in the experiments. Several explanations are possible for this aggravating situation. One explanation is that in spite of what are considered to be adequate controls, different observers may in some subtle way be noting some aspect of the local geometry of the stimulus patterns and cueing in on this aspect of the stimulus rather than the global shape cue we wish them to use. Such local cueing would be very much more difficult to do in a set of stimuli based upon the same stimulus-form (i.e., generated by the same polynominal equation than in a mixed set of different forms).

A second possible explanation is more psychologically subtle. It may be that the explanation is, in the words of Peterson (1986) some "nonstimulus contributions to the perceptual organization" of the stimulus-form utilized here. That is, perhaps the processes being assayed in this study are not as totally preattentive as we think. Perhaps different observers "perceptually organize" the stimuli in different ways and this organization breaks through to influence their visual response. Others (e.g., Haber, 1966; Hochberg & Peterson, 1985; Kahneman & Triesman, 1984) have also suggested this possibility for what otherwise appears to be very low level perceptual processes.

Disconcertingly, both of these speculative answers, as well as most others that could be invoked to explain the present data, are framed in terms of the observer's cognition and of higher level mechanisms than I have tended to invoke in my theories of this kind of form perception. Is the difficulty to

---

[10]Recent personal discussions with Brian Rogers of Oxford University suggest that stereoscopic vision experiments, in particular, are subject to a great deal of variability from task to task, from observer to observer, and from condition to condition. It may be that this reflects either some higher level intervention or the increased difficulty of the task. No general answer to this problem is known at the present time.

which I have alluded a matter of individual differences or idiosyncratic cognitive mechanisms rather than the automatic stimulus-driven preattentive processes I believe are dominant here? I cannot answer this question: I can only report that in every instance in which I have invented some strategy to seek closure or completion in this work, it has turned out that the situation is far more complicated than it had seemed and it has not been achieved.

Thus, there were variations of several different kinds in the obtained results from the several different experiments. These variations illustrate, once again, the fact that general or universal rules seem to be absent in this type of perceptual research and that slight changes in procedure can often have dramatic effects on the outcome of what seem at first glance to be very closely related experiments.

There is, however, one reliable result that has been obtained and that is the main issue to be considered in the remainder of this discussion. That result is the subtle form effect that was obtained from the error matrices for the randomly sampled stimuli in the discrimination and recognition experiments. Prior to this discovery, any stable effect of stimulus-form had proved to be extremely elusive when we looked only at the raw "percentage correct as a function of form" graphs.

The stable[11] form effect that has now been uncovered in these error matrices can be summarized as follows: there are three clusters of confusion errors containing; (a) the arch, cylinder, and saddle; (b) the hemisphere and paraboloid of rotation; and (c) the two cubics and the plane, respectively. (The pattern of interactions within group (c) is complicated by the lack of interaction between the plane and the one dimensional cubic — all other interactions are symmetrical and mutual.) These are the basic psychophysical facts describing this form effect: Our goal is to explain why this should be the case.

The search for an explanation of the forces clustering these eight stimuli into these three clusters led Ramakrishna Kakarala, Nancy Davis, and myself to consider a number of different mathematical approaches. All of the potential models were based upon the idea that there was some kind of similarity among the members of the three clusters that could account for their being interconfused with each other. This premise leads immediately to the idea of some kind of a correlational measure that might explain why the specific shapes cluster together as they do. The first attempt at developing such a correlational explanatory model, therefore, was a simple-minded extrapolation of the autocorrelational model that had proved so powerful in the early two-dimensional studies of detection carried out by this laboratory. This extrapolation consisted of a cross correlation in three-dimensional space of all combinations of the eight forms including self-autocorrelations. Mathematically, this discrete spatial cross correlation identifies regions of intersection

---

[11]But, once again, see Footnote 9.

of the two spatial surfaces being cross correlated. While this analysis produced a very beautiful and colorful set of four-dimensional cross correlograms (the cross correlation of two three-dimensional surfaces produces a solution at each point in a three-space defined by the three axes of shifting $-\Delta x$, $\Delta y$, $\Delta z-$ that was represented by a false color code) there was no attribute, parameter, or aggregate figure of merit of the resulting transformation that we were able to construct that was able to predict the clustering: Neither maximum values, the number of maximum values, nor any other property of the outcome of the transformation or comparison of the geometries of three-dimensional stimuli was able to explain why some of these forms "looked alike" more than others and, were, therefore, confused with each other.

We next applied differential geometry and considered the curvature of the various surfaces with which we were working. Here again no success was achieved; there was no pattern of similarity in simple measures of the curvature nor of such esoteric measures as the Gaussian curvature of the surfaces that had been utilized that could account for the observed confusions.

Our next attempt was to carry out some geometrical gymnastics that were intuitively correlative in nature but not formal cross correlations. Specifically, it was hypothesized that two surfaces would be more "alike" than another pair if the *volume between them* was less than that between the other pair. The *volume-between* concept was implemented by mathematically sliding the two surfaces (which were always in a fronto-parallel orientation — see Figure 6) past each other along the $z$, or depth, axis. Thus, for each pair of stimulus-forms there would be a point in the translation at which the two surfaces would enclose a minimum volume. Unfortunately, neither the raw volume measures obtained in this manner nor any arithmetic transformation of them displayed any attribute or property that could be associated with the origin of the three confusion clusters.

The one predictor that we did find that was successful in classifying the eight stimuli into the three confusion clusters produces a surprising, and admittedly, still incomplete explanation — but it does work very well to provide an alternative way of looking at the outcome of our experiments. This analogous classification (which should hardly at this point be dignified by being called a model) was discovered in the realm of elementary solid analytic geometry. Full discussions of this taxonomy of surfaces can be found in the classic work on geometry by Hilbert and Cohn-Vossen (1932/52) and in the encyclopedia of mathematics edited by Gellert, Kustner, Hellwich, and Kastner (1975).

In brief, solid geometers distinguish between surfaces on the following bases. One major distinction is made among first, second, and third order surfaces. If one considers the stimulus-forms used in this study, the plane is a first order surface, the two cubics are third order, and all others are second order. Within this classification, a further distinction is made between

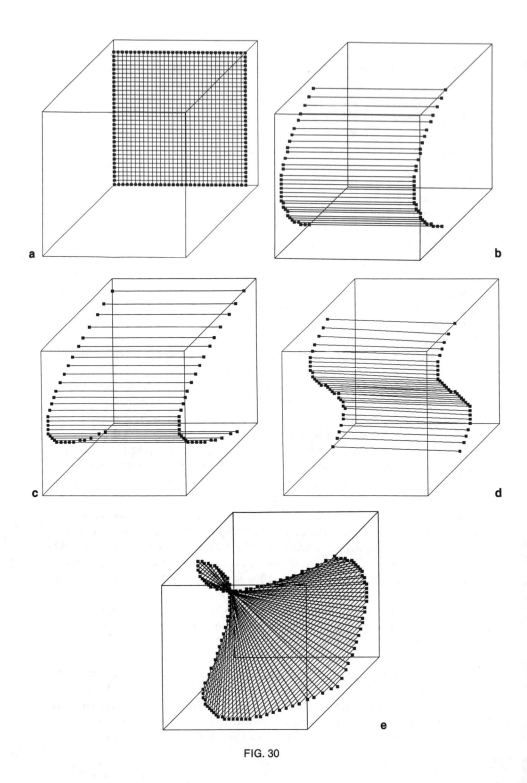

a

b

c

d

e

FIG. 30

"ruled" and "unruled" surfaces; that is, between surfaces that can be constructed from an assemblage of straight lines and those that cannot be so constructed. (The main ruled-unruled dichotomy in which we are interested is for second order surfaces, but third order surfaces can also be ruled or unruled, and the first order plane and the second order saddle are classified as "doubly ruled.") The ruled second order surfaces are the cylinder, the arch, and, somewhat unexpectedly, the hyperbolic paraboloid or saddle. The unruled second order surfaces are the hemisphere and the paraboloid of rotation. The ruled surfaces are shown in Figure 30a-e.

A simple taxonomy of the surfaces can therefore be constructed:

1.  First order surfaces
       The Plane
2.  Second Order Surface
       a.   Ruled Surfaces
               The Cylinder
               The Arch
               The Saddle
       b.   Unruled Surfaces
               The Hemisphere
               The Paraboloid of Rotation
3.   Third order Surfaces
               The One-Dimensional Cubic
               The Two-Dimensional Cubic

The fascinating thing about this geometry-based taxonomy is that the emerging groups of forms are exactly the same as the clusters that were observed in the error matrices from the discrimination and recognition experiments with but one exception. That exception is the confusion that exists between the plane surface and the two-dimensional cubic. This is probably due to the fact that the plane is an exceptionally unstable surface in a mathematical sense in that it can be disrupted by a very small number of extraneous dots. Thus, when embedded among even a modest number of masking dots, it tends towards an irregular surface that is most closely approximated by the irregular surface of the two-dimensional cubic. Other than this exception, the confusions are predicted by the geometrical taxonomy.

That the psychophysical data and the geometric classification should correspond so closely is still not entirely satisfying, of course. There is no mechanistic or reductionistic explanation of why these clusters of surfaces should form in the psychophysical data and, without doubt, the ruled-unruled,

---

FIG. 30   (facing page) Projective drawings of the five ruled surfaces used as stimulus-forms in this study. a. Plane. b. Cylinder. c. Parabolic Arch. d. One-dimensional Cubic. e. Saddle. The actual stimuli contained neither the ruling lines nor the outline cube. They are presented here only to help the reader visualize the shapes of these stimulus-forms.

second-third order, taxonomy reflects something about the geometrical surfaces to which our observers are sensitive that is above and beyond the bare geometrical facts of ruling and order.

In sum, whatever the actual underlying mechanisms, the classification system emerging from studies of solid analytic geometry closely mirrors the psychophysical data. While we cannot say exactly what is the deeper significance of this relationship, it is a possible heuristic to guide our investigations in the future. Other experiments will have to be carried out to confirm the association (there are other surfaces that can be identified within this same geometrical taxonomy that might be added to our list of potential stimulus-forms for future experiments). For the moment, this curious association is presented as an outcome that may stimulate further thought about the relationship between the perceptual and geometrical worlds.

In conclusion we are now able to provide a partial answer to some of the questions that were asked at the beginning of Chapter 3.

1.  An effect of stimulus-form in the dotted-surface in dotted-noise paradigm is to be found in the clusters of confusion errors rather than in the raw percentage correct data. The effect is not totally explicable, but does seem to reflect the solid analytic geometry of the stimulus-forms. Though subtle, there is definitely an effect of form.

2.  There is a substantial difference in the influence of the actual and the apparent signal-to-noise ratio. Stimulus detectability, discriminability, and recognizability follow the actual physical stimulus-form and masking dot densities and the subjective masking dot density. They do not, however, vary as expected as a function of the subjective stimulus-form dot density that can be manipulated by alterations in the disparities of the constituent dots.

3.  There appears to be a serial hierarchy of task in which detection, discrimination, and recognition successively require more information for equivalent performance. The three tasks are not carried out in parallel.

4.  Regularly sampled stimulus-forms are perceived better than randomly sampled ones—in contradiction to our earlier results (Uttal, 1985).

5.  When one changes from two-dimensional to three-dimensional experimental designs, there is a vast change in the nature of the results. Models that worked in the former case do not in the latter and different rules seem to apply.

Finally, I reiterate one of the main metaprinciples that characterizes this work—*The Rule of Multiple Rules: Great changes in results can occur with very small changes in procedure.* In sum, there seem to be few general or universal rules operating within the domain we defined at the outset of this monograph. It is my hope that this is an expression of the early stage of this work and not a fundamental limitation on convergence towards a unified theory of dotted form perception.

# Appendix A
# A Recantation of the Rule of Random Sampling

It is earnestly hoped by every investigator in any science that he will not have to withdraw claims made previously as his work progresses. However, in any study in which data variation (for any one of a large number of reasons) requires that statistical tests be used or in which many different variables must be controlled, there is always a possibility that something observed in one instance will not be obtained in another. This appendix presents one example of a situation in which replication, stimulated by an inconsistent outcome in a cross-checking condition between Experiment 4 and earlier results, leads me to withdraw an earlier claim.

The purpose of this section is to apologize and recant — to correct the previous misinformation and, to the extent possible, analyze how I arrived at the erroneous conclusion. Although the results were potentially interesting, they were unfortunately incorrect. Furthermore, the new results are both less surprising and less interesting.

The specific claim to be withdrawn was summarized in my earlier work (Uttal, 1985) as the Rule of Random Sampling. Two sets of experiments were carried out using the detection task and identical stimulus-forms constructed from either regular (grid arrangement) or randomly placed stimuli. The empirical result was very strong. Figures 31 and 32 show the outcome of a typical experiment in which a one-dimensional cubic form was presented to a group of observers in a regularly or randomly sampled version respectively. The two sets of data show a dramatic difference between the detectability scores in the two experiments — the regularly sampled data, though initially more detectable, actually became substantially less detectable as the masking dot density increased. This was a highly interesting, though counterintuitive, outcome since the advantage exhibited by random sampling was in the direc-

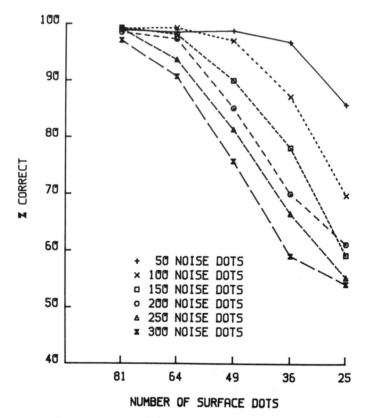

FIG. 31    The results of Supplementary Experiment 14 from Uttal (1985) in which it originally appeared that there was a substantial disadvantage in the *detectability* of regular over random forms. These data are for the regular forms.

tion opposite to that expected on the basis of a known artifact. This experiment had been acknowledged to be flawed in that earlier report by being classified as a "supplementary" experiment. The difficulty was that the regularly sampled stimuli were contaminated with a monocular cue; the lines of stimulus dots could be detected with a single eye. As Figure 33 shows, however, the difference between the stereograms for a regularly sampled three-dimensional surface and for an array of randomly positioned (in three-dimensional space) dots was not complete—lines of dots were present in the random (in position) stimulus as well as in the one defining a surface.

Even more compelling in support of the data, flawed as the experiment was known to be, was the fact that the performance curves actually crossed over. At the lower masking dot densities observers all performed better in the regular than in the random sample situation. At the higher masking dot densities, however, the disadvantage of the regularly sampled surfaces became substantial. This characteristic of the curves representing the performance of the observer, coupled with the fact that in every experiment that was carried out attacking this problem (five in all), the results were the same, led me to confidently express the rule that detection was better with randomly than with regularly sampled stimuli in spite of this monocular confounding. Indeed, the monocular confounding, if it had been influential, should have driven the results in the direction producing an advantage for the regular stimuli. Because our results went in the opposite direction, giving the advantage to the randomly sampled stimulus-forms, rather than that predicted by the known monocular confounding, the results were interesting and tantalizingly acceptable. (Incidentally, any regularly sampled stimuli will display this same monocular confounding.)

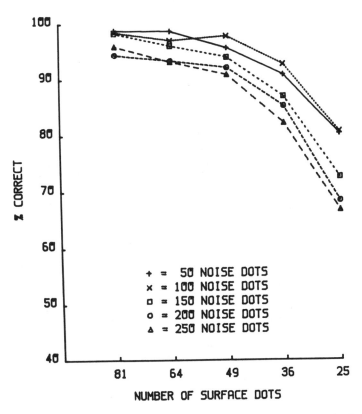

FIG. 32    The results of Experiment 7 from Uttal (1985) showing the results for the detectability of randomly sampled stimuli. These data were compared with the result in Figure 31 to produce the now discredited Rule of Random Sampling. The data are plotted as a function of the number of dots on the one-dimensional cubic surface and are parametric across the number of masking dots.

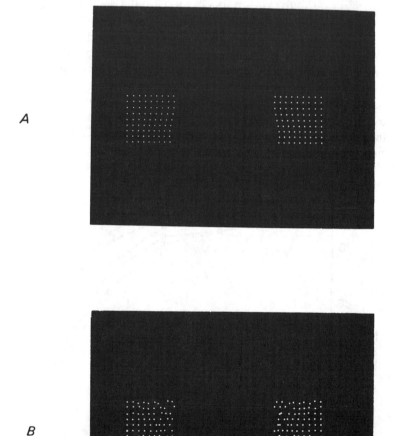

*A*

*B*

FIG. 33    Examples of regularly sampled stimuli showing the relatively modest differences between stimuli when the dots are constrained to a cubic surface (a) and when the dots possess random z coordinates (b).

To add to the misdirection, a theoretical explanation was discovered that supported the erroneous empirical results and strongly supported their veracity. Statistical sampling theory had for many years provided rigorous proofs that random sampling was more effective in reproducing three-dimensional shapes if the shapes had a high "autocorrelation"; i.e., if the shapes were such that nearby points on the surface were more likely to be alike than distant ones.

With all of this misdirection, it was all too easy to see how I could arrive at this misconclusion. The error began to unravel in Experiment 4 (a similar, but not an identical detection experiment) in which regularly and randomly sampled stimuli were compared. The main difference between this experiment and the supplementary experiments in Uttal (1985) is that in the original experiments only a single form of varying curvature had been used, whereas in Experiment 4 the set of different forms shown in Figure 6, each of maximum curvature, had been used. However, this experiment did contain several conditions that were equivalent to those used in the earlier supplemental experiments — and our observers did not behave on those conditions as they had in the original experiments. In all cases, the randomly sampled stimuli were less easily detected than were the regularly sampled ones.

To determine if this was a result of the differing experimental designs — perhaps the spurious counterintuitive superiority of randomly over regularly sampled stimuli was a result of the fact that in the original supplementary experiments only one stimulus-form had been used in each experiment — the original experimental design was replicated. The important new variable, we were later to discover, was that only one group of observers was used in *both* parts of the comparison. The experiment was replicated only for the one-dimensional cubic stimuli but was identical in all other regards to the design of Experiment 7 and supplementary experiment 14 in Uttal (1985).

The results of this replication of the detection experiment for the one-dimensional cubic stimulus-forms are shown in Figures 34, 35, and 36. In Figure 34 the results are plotted for the randomly sampled stimuli as a function of stimulus-form dot density parametric in the masking dot density. The same plan is used to present the data for the regularly sampled stimuli in Figure 35. In each of these figures, the data are pooled across all degrees of stimulus curvatures just as they were in the original experiment as shown in Figures 31 and 32.

Figure 36 summarizes what should be obvious in Figures 34 and 35. The data here are pooled further across all of the masking dot densities and plotted together to show the relation between the observers' performance for the two kinds of stimulus forms. Clearly, regularity helps, rather than hinders, in this task and the previous results were wrong.

There is a double-barreled loss here. Not only was the conclusion wrong, but the outcome that we now believe to be the true case is simply not very in-

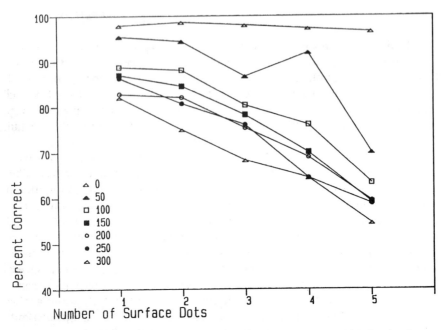

FIG. 34    The results of the replication of Experiment 7 from Uttal (1984) showing the *detectability* of randomly sampled forms. the data are plotted as a function of the number of dots in the stimulus-form with the code numbers 1 = 81; 2 = 64; 3 = 49; 4 = 36; and 5 = 25 dots.

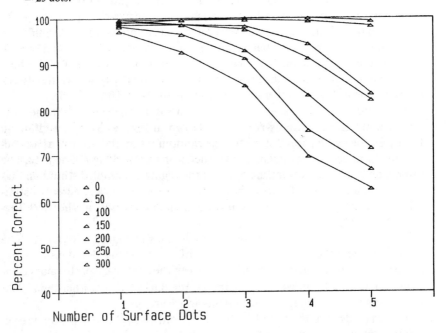

FIG. 35    The results of the replication of Supplementary Experiment 14 showing the *detectability* of regularly sampled stimulus-forms. The code for the horizontal axis is the same as in Figure 33.

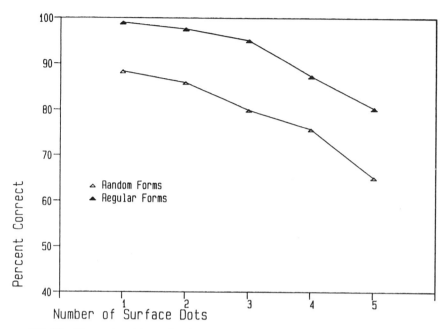

**FIG. 36**    The results of the replication experiments pooled and plotted as a function of the number of dots in the stimulus form show the advantage of detectability of the regularly sampled forms over the randomly sampled forms.

teresting. The result *was* interesting when it ran counter to direction predicted by the known monocular artifact. However, it is now impossible to determine how much of the advantage of regularity can be attributed to its stereoscopic three-dimensionality and how much to the monocular "rule of linear periodicity." This lack of excitement transposes to Experiment 4, 5, and 6 of the present work as well.

How could the mismeasurement that was obtained in the 1985 volume have occurred? I now believe that it can be accounted for by the fact that *different groups of observers* had been used in the randomly sampled and regularly sampled experiments respectively. In retrospect, we must accept the fact that the set of observers used in the latter experiment were simply not as good as those used in the former one. The erroneous result, therefore, is attributable to a sampling error. This embarrassing turn of events stresses the importance of using exactly the same group of observers whenever comparisons of different conditions are made. Indeed, all important comparisons should be made within the confines of the same set of sessions and using the same observers, if at all possible. While this advice is a truism at this point, individual differences, though known to be substantial, had not been thought to produce such qualitatively erroneous results. How I wish they had been!

# References

Appelle, S. Perception and discrimination as a function of stimulus orientation: The "oblique effect" in man and animals. *Psychological Bulletin,* 1972, *78,* 266–278.

Beck, S., Prazdny, K., & Rosenfeld, A. A theory of textural segmentation. In J. Beck, B. Hope, & A. Rosenfeld (Eds.), *Human and machine vision.* New York: Academic Press, 1983.

Brunswik, E. The conceptual framework of psychology. In *International encyclopedia of unified science* (Vol. 1; No. 10). Chicago: University of Chicago Press, 1952.

Brunswik, E. *Perception and the representative design of psychological experiments* (2nd ed.). Berkeley: University of California Press, 1956.

Campbell, D. T., & Stanley, J. *Experimental and quasi-experimental designs for research.* Chicago: Rand-McNally, 1966.

Coffin, S. Spatial frequency analysis of block letters does not predict experimental confusions. *Perception & Psychophysics,* 1978, *23,* 69–74.

Cronbach, L. J. Beyond the two disciplines of scientific psychology. *American Psychologist,* 1975, *30*(2), 116–127.

Daugman, J. G. Spatial visual channels in fourier plane. *Vision Research,* 1984, *24* (9), 891–910.

Descartes, R. [Discourse on the method, Part III] In E. S. Haldane & G. T. R. Ross (Eds. & trans.), *The philosophical works of Descartes.* Cambridge, England: Cambridge University Press, 1967. (Originally published, 1637).

Diener, D. On the relationship between detection and recognition. *Perception & Psychophysics,* 1981, *30* (3), 237–246.

Doehrman, S. The effect of visual orientation uncertainty in a simultaneous detection recognition task. *Perception & Psychophysics,* 1974, *15,* 519–523.

Einhorn, H. J., & Hogarth, R. M. Behavioral decision theory: Processes of judgment and choice. *Annual Review of Psychology,* 1981, *32,* 53–88.

Epstein, S. The stability of behavior: I. On predicting most of the people much of the time. *Journal of Personality and Social Psychology,* 1979, *37,* 1097–1126.

Epstein, S. The stability of behavior: II. Implications for psychological research. *American Psychologist,* 1980, *35,* 790–806.

Furcher, C. S., Thomas, J. P., & Campbell, F. W. Detection and discrimination of simple and complex patterns at low spatial frequencies. *Vision Research,* 1977, *17,* 827–836.

Garner, W. R. *The processing of information and structure.* Hillsdale, NJ: Lawrence Erlbaum Associates, 1974.

Gellert, W., Kustner, H., Hellwich, M., & Kastner, H. (Eds.), *The VNR concise encyclopaedia of mathematics.* New York: Van Nostrand Reinhold, 1975.

Glass, L., & Switkes, E. Pattern recognition in humans: Correlations which cannot be perceived. *Perception,* 1976, *5,* 67–72.

Goldmeier, E. Limits of visibility of bronchogenic carcinoma. *The American Review of Respiratory Diseases,* February 1965, *91,* (2) 232–239.

Goldmeier, E. Similarity in visually perceived forms. *Psychological Issues,* 1972, *8* (whole #9). (Originally published, 1936).

Grassman, H. Zur theories der farbenmischung. *Pogg. Ann. Physik.,* 8, 89, 69; *Phil. Mag.,* (Serv. 4), 1853, *7,* 254.

Green, D. M., & Birdsall, T. G. Detection and recognition. *Psychological Review,* 1978, *85,* 192–205.

Greenwald, A. G. Significance, nonsignificance, and interpretation of an ESP experiment. *Journal of Experimental Social Psychology,* 1975, *11,* 180–191.

Greenwald, A. G. Within-subjects design: To use or not to use? *Psychological Bulletin,* 1976, *83,* 314–320.

Gregory, R. L., & Heard, P. Border locking and Café Wall illusion. *Perception,* 1979, *8,* 365–380.

Grimson, W. E. L. *From images to surfaces. A computational study of the human early visual system.* Cambridge, MA: The MIT Press, 1981.

Grossberg, S. The quantized geometry of visual space: The coherent computation of depth, form, and lightness. *Behavioral & Brain Sciences,* 1983, *6,* 625–692.

Grossberg, S., & Mingolla, E. Neural dynamics of perceptual grouping: Textures; boundaries, and emergent segmentations. *Perception & Psychophysics,* 1985, *38* (2), 141–171.

Haber, R. N. Nature of the effect of set on perception. *Psychological Review,* 1966, *73,* 335–351.

Haig, N. D. How faces differ — A new comparative technique. *Perception,* 1985, *14,* 601–615.

Hammond, K. R. *The psychology of Egon Brunswik.* New York: Holt, Rinehart, & Winston, 1966.

Hammond, K. R., Hamm, R. M., & Grassia, J. Generalizing over conditions by combining the multitrait multimethod matrix and the representative design of experiments. *Psychological Bulletin,* (in press).

Hilbert, D., & Cohn-Vossen, S. *Geometry and the imagination.* New York: Chelsea, 1932/1952.

Hochberg, J., & Peterson, M. A. *Perceptual couples as measures of the role of local cues and intention in form perception.* Unpublished manuscript, 1985.

Hurvich, L. M., Jameson, D., & Krantz, D. H. Theoretical treatments of selected visual problems. *Handbook of mathematical psychology.* New York: Wiley, 1965.

Jenkins, J. Remember that old theory of memory? Well, forget it! *American Psychologist,* 1974, *29,* 785–795.

Julesz, B. Binocular depth perception of computer-generated patterns. *Bell System Tech. J.,* 1960, *39,* 1125–1162.

Julesz, B. *Foundations of cyclopean perception.* Chicago: The University of Chicago Press, 1971.

Julesz, B. Textons, the elements of perception, and their interactions. *Nature,* 1981, *290,* 91–97.

Julesz, B., & Chang, J. J. Do hypercyclopean textons exist? *Investigative Ophthalmology and Visual Science,* 1984, *25,* 199.

Kahneman, D., & Triesman, A. Changing views of attention and automaticity. In R. Parasuraman & J. Beatty (Eds.), *Varieties of attention.* New York: Academic Press, 1984.

Kas, J. H. The segregation of function in the nervous system: Why do sensory systems have so many subdivisions? *Sensory Physiology,* 1982, *7,* 201–240.

Kincaid, W., & Uttal, W. R. The effect of 3-D orientation and stretching on the detection of dotted planes. *Perception and psychophysics,* 1986, *39,* 392–396.

Klein, R. M., & Barresi, J. Perceptual saliance of form versus material as a function of variation in spacing and number of elements. *Perception and Psychophysics,* 1985, *37,* 440–446.

Koch, S. Epilogue. In S. Koch (Ed.), *Psychology: A study of a science* (Vol. 3; pp. 729–788). New York: McGraw-Hill, 1959.

Korte, A. Kinematoskopische Untersuchungen. *Zeitschrift für Psychologie,* 1915, *72,* 193–296.

Lappin, J., Langston, A., & Livert, D. Investigative ophthalmology & visual science. *ARVO Abstracts,* March 1984, *25.*

Marr, D. *Vision. A computational investigation into the human representation and processing of visual information.* San Francisco, CA: W. H. Freeman, 1982.

Marr, D., & Poggio, T. A computational theory of human stereo vision. *Proc. R. Soc. Long.,* 1979, *B204,* 301–328.

Mayhew, J. E. W. Stereopsis. In O. J. Braddick & A. C. Sleigh (Eds.), *Physical and biological processing of images* (pp. 204–216). Berlin, Federal Republic of Germany: Springer-Verlag, 1982.

Mayhew, J. E. W., & Frisby, J. P. Psychophysical and computational studies towards a theory of human stereopsis. *Artificial Intelligence,* 1981, *17,* 349–387.

Meehl, P. E. Theoretical risks and tabular asterisks: Sir Karl, Sir Ronald, and the slow process of soft psychology. *Journal of Consulting and Clinical Psychology,* 1978, *46,* 806–834.

Mill, John Stuart. Essay on Bentham in F. R. Leavis (Ed.), *Mill on Bentham and Coleridge,* (Chapter 4). Chatto & Windus, 1838/1950.

Navon, D. Forest before trees: The presence of global features in visual perception. *Cognitive Psychology,* 1977, *9,* 353–383.

Neisser, U. *Cognition and reality. Principles and implications of cognitive psychology.* San Francisco, CA: W. H. Freeman, 1976.

Nolte, L. W. Theory of signal detectability: Adaptive optimum receiver design. *Journal of the Acoustical Society of America,* 1967, *42,* 773–777.

Northdurft, H. C. Texture discrimination does not occur at the cyclopean retina. *Perception,* 1985, *14,* 527–537.

Parasuraman, R., & Beatty, J. Brain events underlying detection and recognition of weak sensory signals. *Science,* 1980, *3,* 80–83.

Peterson, M. A. Illusory concomitant motion in ambiguous stereograms: Evidence for nonstimulus contributions to perceptual organization. *Journal of Experimental Psychology: Human Perception and Performance,* 1986, *12* (1), 50–60.

Ramachandran, V. S. The neurobiology of perception. *Perception,* 1985, *14,* 97–103.

Sagi, D., & Julesz, B. "Where" and "what" in vision. *AT&T Bell Laboratories.* Murray Hill, NJ, 1985.

Shepard, R. N. Attention and the metric structure of the stimulus space. *Journal of Mathematical Psychology,* 1964, *1,* 54–87.

Simon, H. A. *Models of thought.* New Haven: Yale University Press, 1979.

Sperling, G. Mathematical models of binocular vision. In *Mathematical psychology and psychophysiology,* S. Grossberg (Ed.). Providence, RI: American Mathematical Society, 1981.

Starr, S. J., Metz, C. F., Lusted, L. B., & Goodenough, D. J. Visual detection and localization of radiographic images. *Radiology,* 1975, *116,* 533–538.

Stevens, K. A. Autocorrelation has no merit in 3–D, figuratively. *Contemporary Psychology,* 1986, *31,* (1), 23–24.

Swets, J. A., Green, D. M., Getty, D. J., & Swets, J. B. Signal detection and identification at successive stages of observation. *Perception & Psychophysics,* 1978, *23* (4), 275–289.

Thomas, J. P., Gille, J., & Barker, R. A. Simultaneous visual detection and identification: Theory and data. *Journal of the Ophthalmology Society of America,* December 1982, *72* (12), 1642–1650.

Triesman, A. Perceptual grouping and attention in visual search for objects. *Journal of Experi-*

*mental Psychology: Human Perception and Performance,* 1982, *8* (2), 194–214.

Triesman, A., & Gelade, G. A feature-integration theory of attention. *Cognitive Psychology,* 1980, *12,* 97–136.

Triesman, A., & Patterson, R. Emergent features, attention, and object perception. *Journal of Experimental Psychology: Human Perception and Performance,* 1984, *10* (1), 12–31.

Triesman, A., & Schmidt, H. Illusory conjuctions in the perception of objects. *Cognitive Psychology,* 1982, *14,* 107–141.

Triesman, A., Skyes, M., & Gelade, G. Selective attention and stimulus integration. In S. Dornic (Ed.), *Attention and performance,* (Vol. 6; pp. 333–361). Hillsdale, NJ: Lawrence Erlbaum Associates, 1977.

Triesman, A., & Souther, J. Search asymmetry: A diagnostic for preattentive processing of separable features. University of British Columbia, Canada, 1986.

Tulving, E. Memory research: What kind of progress? In L. G. Nilsson (Ed.), *Perspectives in memory research,* (pp. 19–34). Hillsdale, NJ: Lawrence Erlbaum Associates, 1979.

Uttal, W. R. *An autocorrelation theory of form detection.* Hillsdale, NJ: Lawrence Erlbaum Associates, 1975.

Uttal, W. R. *A taxonomy of visual process.* Hillsdale, NJ: Lawrence Erlbaum Associates, 1981.

Uttal, W. R. *Visual form detection in 3-dimensional space.* Hillsdale, NJ: Lawrence Erlbaum Associates, 1983.

Uttal, W. R. *The detection of nonplanar surfaces in visual space.* Hillsdale, NJ: Lawrence Erlbaum Associates, 1985.

Uttal, W. R., Fitzgerald, J., & Eskin, T. E. Rotation and translation effects on stereopic acuity. *Vision Research,* 1975, *15,* 939–944.

Van Essen, D. C. Functional organization of primate visual cortex. In A. Peters & E. G. Jones (Eds.), *Cerebral Cortex* (Vol. 3), New York: Plenum, 1985.

Van Tuijl, H. F. J. M. A new visual illusion: Neonlike color spreading and complementary color induction between subjective contours. *Acta Psychol. Amst.,* 1975, *39,* 441–445.

Wagner, M. The metric of visual space. *Perception & Psychophysics,* 1985, *38* (6), 483–495.

Ward, T. B. Individual differences in processing stimulus dimensions: Relation to selective processing abilities. *Perception & Psychophysics,* 1985, *37,* 47–482.

Wertheimer, H. Ennunciation of the Gestalt rules of grouping. *Psychol. Forsch.,* 1922, *1,* 47–58.

Yu, B., Brogan, J., Robertson, S, & Uttal, W. R. The detection of chinese strokes and characters in visual noise. *Perception & Psychophysics,* 1985, *38,* 23–29.

Zeki, S. M. Functional specialization in the visual cortex of the rhesus monkey. *Nature,* 1978, London, *274,* 423–428.

Zeki, S. M. Color coding in the cerebral cortex: The reaction of cells in monkey visual cortex to wavelengths and colors. *Neuroscience,* 1983, *9,* 741–765 (a).

# Author Index

## W

Wagner, M., 8, *108*
Ward, T.B., 6, *108*
Wertheimer, H., 7, *108*

## Y

Yu, B., 29, *108*

## Z

Zeki, S.M., 17, *108*

# Subject Index

## V

Visual processing,
  levels, 3
    attentive, 4, 30, 59, 76, 89
    cognitive, *see* attentive
    discernible, 3
    intermediate, 4, 10, 21
    preattentive, 3, 10, 49, 76, 87, 88–89
    precognitive, *see* preattentive